THE
PARTY
Inside Fianna Fáil

Dick Walsh

Gill and Macmillan

Published in Ireland by
Gill and Macmillan Ltd
Goldenbridge
Dublin 8
with associated companies in
Auckland, Dallas, Delhi, Hong Kong,
Johannesburg, Lagos, London, Manzini,
Melbourne, Nairobi, New York, Singapore,
Tokyo, Washington
©Dick Walsh 1986
5   4   3   2   1
0 7171 1446 5
Print origination in Ireland by Galaxy Reproductions Ltd
Printed in Great Britain by
Richard Clay (The Chaucer Press) Ltd, Bungay, Suffolk.

Contents

Acknowledgments

As I prepared this book I was advised, encouraged and instructed by Michael Mills, Arthur Noonan and my brother, John; other old friends and colleagues among the political correspondents and in the *Irish Times* were as stimulating and helpful as ever. Douglas Gageby and James Downey generously allowed me the time I needed to complete the work; Anthony Lennon (*Irish Times*) and Anne Kenny (Leinster House) shortened that time with their research, as did Claire Hooper with the typescript. Fergal Tobin of Gill and Macmillan provided subtle and imaginative guidance.

Of the politicians and party members who helped, one — John Hanafin, a courtly man who loved and served the country well and was a member of the national executive for many years — must stand for all.

Without my family, in Wicklow, Dublin and Clare, this book would not have been written. Ruth, Francesca and Suzanne lived with it for a year. Here's to them and other animals, not all of them political. . . .

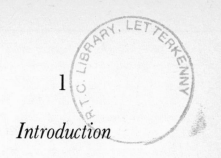

1

Introduction

'We're Fianna Fáil,' said the neighbour, 'and always were. Ever since the Risin'.'

'Since 'Sixteen?' said my father, raising his eyebrows. He was a man who took things literally.

'Since 'Ninety-Eight,' said the neighbour, who knew what every believer knew: there always was a Fianna Fáil and there always would be.

You could hardly have believed otherwise in East Clare during the 'forties without inviting the question: 'Are you Irish at all?' Even my father, who fell out with the party over the teachers' strike in 1946, thought there was something faintly heretical about criticising Dev. 'That kind of thing goes against the grain,' he would say. And in his case it did, for though he had taken to voting for Clann na Poblachta he was all that you might expect of a party man, mixing love of the Irish language with intolerance of anything that was vaguely West British and fierce local pride with passionate support of the GAA, including its ban on foreign games. History was not so much a matter of learning from the past as of stirring old grievances to keep them on the boil: if only we'd met Cromwell on the way home, we'd have made short work of him; we knew how Dan O'Connell, the Liberator, had said he'd drive a coach and four through the laws of a British parliament – and, by God, he did – and that Robert Emmet's dying word had been that when Ireland took her place among the nations of

1

the earth, then and not until then, should his epitaph be written. To which my father always added: 'Poor Emmet.' There was more than a hint of unfinished business.

Our history asked no questions. Officially, it stopped safely short of the Civil War. My father included an entirely unofficial account of the East Clare Flying Column which had loped through the hills and woods around us — woods, mark you, that had sheltered Brian Boru long before the British took their great oaks by the shipload for the re-roofing of Westminster Abbey. We were never, officially or otherwise, brought face to face with the State we lived in or with the ironies and contradictions with which its history was resonant. The party was never mentioned though, it now seems, all that we learned was nudging us firmly in its direction. That may have been inevitable, for we were living not only in de Valera's constituency but in the heart of what, by then, had become a Fianna Fáil State.

Of all the ironies and contradictions, none was stranger than the way in which the losers of the Civil War, once they had come to power in the 'thirties, made their own of a State they had so desperately opposed. But they did make their own of it, and with such success that for a long time the occasional break in their rule was to seem like a period of rest and recuperation for the party or a barely excusable lapse on the part of the people. Some had feared that it would be otherwise, if and when de Valera won an election. A professor in the Cumann na nGaedheal stronghold of University College, Dublin was to admit that he and his colleagues expected the country to be plunged into 'Mexican politics' — by which he meant that the Civil War would be resumed, this time with communist and anti-clerical forces opposing the supporters of law-and-order and the bishops. He was wrong. The smoothness of the transfer of power, in spite of the activities of the IRA and, later, the Blueshirts, was a tribute to the maturity of both sides and to the strength of the democratic foundations laid by Cumann na nGaedheal

2

and defended at such terrible cost. In the end, not only did the new party fit comfortably the contours of the State; the State in many respects came to resemble the party.

How and why the role of rightful heir was assumed by Fianna Fáil is a question for any account, not only of the party but of the country during the past sixty years. For, since 1932, Fianna Fáil has not ceased to be the most popular of Irish parties. Its support in general elections has never fallen below 40 per cent and twice was over 50 per cent; it has governed alone, or with a little help from minority groups or independents, for almost forty of the past fifty-four years, and its Presidential candidates have invariably been successful. Few parties can touch that record: the Social Democrats in Sweden, Christian Democrats in Italy, Nationalists in South Africa and Unionists in Northern Ireland.

The party's leaders, from Eamon de Valera to Charlie Haughey, could well describe the crowds at their ard-fheiseanna as the most representative assemblies of Irish nationalists since the heyday of Sinn Féin. Fianna Fáil has always been supported by as many of the rich as Fine Gael and by more of the poor than Labour though, by the middle of the 'eighties, its electoral appeal was strongest among older, more conservative voters than those who backed either of its major opponents.

In defining the party's attractions there can be no short cuts; Fianna Fáil itself shies away from precise definitions. De Valera once said: 'Always keep your policy under your hat,' and that was what he did. So unaccustomed was the party to making written commitments that when Seán Lemass produced his First Programme for Economic Expansion in the late 'fifties, some of his parliamentary colleagues tried to suggest that it was the work of civil servants. Twenty years later a disastrous election manifesto, which ironically contributed to the party's greatest electoral triumph, was to convince the sceptics that de Valera had been right. Pro-

3

grammatic politics had no place in a populist movement.

Fianna Fáil was, from the start, as much a movement as a party. Relying on tradition, emotion, a particular view of the past, it was built on simple beliefs: in the national cause, which embraced unity and the restoration of Irish; in self-sufficiency, based on the land and other native resources; and in the integrity of small communities, whose borders were conveniently coterminus with those of the Catholic Church and the GAA. The beliefs were vague enough to hold a universal appeal: no-one need feel excluded. But at the core of the movement lay the party — secretive, disciplined and controlled with almost military precision, dedicated to its leader and under his leadership to winning and wielding power. As a classic populist leader, de Valera fitted the bill to a T. At his best, speaking for small nations as president of the League of Nations or in his calm and dignified reply to Winston Churchill at the end of the Second World War, he seemed to speak from the heart of every Irish citizen. At his most contradictory, he infuriated his opponents and bewildered his friends.

Inevitably, the party bore his contradictions as its own; it simply ignored them. At the height of his anti-clerical reputation in the 'twenties, he consulted a theologian on the Oath that blocked the party's path to the Dáil, until he discovered that it was an 'empty formula'. His dilemma became the subject of a learned Jesuitical paper. He went a step further and consulted the Pope about the constitution; and in the 'fifties he silently observed the conflict between the bishops and Noel Browne over the Mother and Child Scheme, then moved in and took advantage of the chaos it had caused. De Valera, who had been solemnly condemned by the bishops during the Civil War, took these changes in his stride. The party, uncomplaining, followed in his wake. Whatever their leader's reasons for changing course — personal devotion to Catholicism or a desire to prove that he and his party were as Catholic as the rest — they recognised his shrewd instinct for the main political chance and knew that, without him, they were lost. He was, however, in some respects like a laity-ridden priest who finds it difficult to get his congregation to differentiate between what he says — and means — and what they believe him to have said because they think they know what he means. True, his convoluted style could make his reasoning hard to follow and occasionally the ambivalence seemed designed to keep all sides happy; but he was clearly opposed to physical force, had adopted a gradualist approach to unity and recognised the failure of his vision of a rural society long before some of his more enthusiastic supporters were prepared to admit any of these things.

The party that he did so much to shape emerged from its mould as a Catholic, nationalist organisation, confused about force but definitely confined to the twenty-six counties. It had a keen sense of self-preservation and was deeply embedded in a community which, since the reforms of the nineteenth century, had come to place a high value on the private ownership of land and property. Its education and health services were largely in the hands of the Catholic Church, which was relieved to discover that the party was not going to live up to its radical reputation, but to concentrate on the national myths and symbols that would in time find a place with the more overtly religious pieties in every right-thinking Irishman's heart.

The party proved capable of living with odd bedfellows, welcoming support from whatever quarter it came. Paddy Belton, one of the founders of a Fine Gael dynasty, was among its first TDs; he was expelled for taking his seat before the rest of his colleagues. James Dillon, that most eloquent of Fine Gael leaders (he was not to join the party until much later), voted for de Valera in 1932. Noel Browne became a member of Fianna Fáil after the disintegration of the Inter-Party government in 1951. One of Haughey's administrations in the 'eighties survived, if only briefly, with the support of the Marxist Workers' Party; the same administration was more

5

than usually accommodating to the bishops and the Catholic fundamentalists who ran campaigns in favour of writing a prohibition on abortion into the constitution and against the liberalisation of the law on contraception. Odd bedfellows, indeed, especially when Browne's membership is recalled — and the dash of radicalism which once attracted the attention of two other unlikely admirers, Conor Cruise O'Brien and Justin Keating.

Most members, however, were born into the party, their loyalty, like their religion, taken for granted. Disloyalty was as unthinkable as treason. The penalty, because movement and nation were one, was expulsion from the moral community. To be considered anti-national was to be thought beyond redemption, a sanction which even the bishops might envy. Three times in thirty years, Fianna Fáil faced threats which a less deeply rooted party might not have survived. On each occasion, the loyalty that was bred in the bones ensured that it weathered the storm. In the late 'fifties, the challenge arose from the failure of the vision of self-sufficiency, based on native resources and a rural society. Unemployment, emigration and flight from the land carried the risk of social disintegration. Seán Lemass reversed traditional attitudes to industry and investment and breathed new life into a demoralised State. Ten years later, fighting in the North brought the party face to face with one of its most blatant contradictions — the gap between its rhetoric and the reality of the national question. Jack Lynch was asked to make a choice that was demanded of no other leader; and he chose the path of gradualism inherited from de Valera and Lemass. He protected the State they had come to sustain and held the party intact. In the 'eighties, the challenge came from without and within the party: Haughey faced highly organised opponents on both fronts and responded with a more combative attitude to the North, a sterner line on discipline and greater emphasis on leadership than any of his predecessors. Loyalty took on a new, more personal, meaning.

6

Could such a party, so long in office and so hungry for power, fail to deliver much — if not all — that it had promised? It delivered, but not what it promised, though that has made no difference to its electoral appeal. Fianna Fáil failed to accomplish any of the seven aims it set itself in 1926. Sixty years later they remain unchanged in its constitution. Unity and the restoration of the Irish language are as far away as they have ever been. The ideals of self-sufficiency and keeping people on the land were abandoned after a struggle. No-one has seriously attempted to make the country's resources and wealth 'subservient to the needs and welfare of all the people' and the Democratic Programme of the First Dáil, briefly discussed when it was adopted, has hardly been heard of since. The 'ruralisation of industries' has been tried, but by Pol Pot in Kampuchea and with disastrous results. Unity and the language are still untouchable symbols of national piety; the rest are like relics of old decency, family heirlooms which no-one would dare to throw away.

The party, nevertheless, clings to that certain view of Ireland and its past, a particular, unmistakable, proprietorial view which it shares with no other institution, as Lynch discovered when he was driving an old-timer from Cork city through his favourite countryside around Gougaune Barra. The old man was sitting, morose and unimpressed with mountain or lake until they came to a memorial cross that he hadn't seen before. They were barely stopped when he jumped from the car with a shout: 'Jasus, Jack, who was shot here?' He was disappointed. The memorial was to Saint Finbar and he, alas, did not have a national record. Another old-timer, Jimmy Collins of west Limerick, proved that the party's interests were ever uppermost in its members' minds when, with some other TDs, he was shown around the cathedral in Strasbourg. He made no comment until he got outside and could fix its spacious entrance with the eye of a man who had addressed a thousand after-Mass meetings. Then, with a shake of his head he delivered his expert opinion: 'Begod,

7

lads, it's a great hoor of a chapel.' However idealistic or romantic its view of the past, the party never lost touch with its local roots. A man who had learned his ward-heeling within nodding distance of Tammany Hall in New York travelled the country with a pair of Fianna Fáil's most energetic localists in 1970 and returned to Dublin, bleary-eyed, exhausted and filled with envy. He spread his weary frame over a couple of seats in the Dáil bar and came up with the verdict: 'Some goddam outfit.' We could hardly disagree.

2

A Potted History

The party emerged from two misfortunes that had become all too familiar to Irish nationalists, defeat and dissension. Defeat on the Treaty, in the Civil War, in two elections; dissension over whether republican representatives should take their seats in the Dáil. De Valera proposed that they should, arguing that once the oath of allegiance to the king had been abolished, it would be a question of policy, not of principle. The opposition was led by two people whose dedication to the national cause was beyond doubt: Father Michael O'Flanagan, the self-appointed Pope of the republican movement, as Seán Lemass called him, and Mary McSwiney, the movement's fundamentalist conscience. As they saw it, republican representatives would be tainted by participation in an assembly set up under English law. They favoured abstention, and the delegates at the Sinn Féin ard-fheis were with them. The majority was thin — five votes from a total of 441 — but it was enough to convince de Valera that, for him, it was the end of the road. The movement had chosen the wilderness. More than forty years later, he was to recall how he left the hall in Rathmines on 10 March 1926, determined to quit public life. From now on, he told Lemass, he would devote his energy to the restoration of Irish.

Seán was shocked to hear me saying this. He said: 'But you're not going to leave us now, Dev, at this stage. You can't leave us like that. We have to go on now. We must

9

form a new organisation, along the policy lines you suggested to the ard-fheis. It's the only way forward.' We discussed it further and, at last, I could not but agree to his logic. I said I would do all the necessary things. But we were only a few people and we hadn't a penny between us.

De Valera had a way of getting others to suggest courses that he had already decided on, and on this occasion the decision was not as spontaneous as he made it appear. Lemass had written a year earlier of the need for greater realism in the republicans' approach to politics.

The idea of a new organisation had already taken root. Within a week of the ard-fheis, a group was meeting nightly at de Valera's house in Sandymount to plot its course. The 'old team', he called them; and though they may have been few, and certainly did not have a penny between them, they were the most able of the republicans and the most realistic. Like de Valera himself, they were survivors and they were to remain, through his political career and theirs, his closest colleagues: Frank Aiken, Sean T. O'Kelly, James Ryan, Gerry Boland, P. J. Ruttledge, Tom Derrig, Sean MacEntee and Lemass. They were to be key men in his cabinets and, after Dev, the most influential members of the party. They were 'old warriors' even then, with shared experience in the struggle for independence and the Civil War, but they were still young in years. At 44, de Valera and O'Kelly were elders among them; Aiken was 28, Lemass 26. Whether or not the new party was contemplated before the Sinn Féin split, they lost no time in getting it on the road. Within a month, de Valera was announcing their intentions:

> We believe the republicans ought not to stand aside and allow the country to be utterly ruined, and all except the imperialists [by which he meant the government and its supporters] to be driven out of it. We are convinced, besides, that the ideal of the majority of the Irish people

10

is still broadly the republican ideal — an Ireland united, free and Irish — and that the people can be banded together for the pursuit of that ideal if a reasonable programme based on existing conditions be set before them. We intend at any rate to make trial and see.

Devising a 'reasonable programme based on existing conditions' was the founders' central task. It was the essence of their New Departure. They quickly agreed a set of simple aims and settled on a name, but even before that was done Tommy Mullins, who was to become the party's toughminded general secretary, had set up its first cumann. De Valera listed the aims in an interview given exactly five weeks after the Sinn Féin split. As well as unity and the restoration of Irish, they included the creation of a society of equal opportunity, distribution of land and the development of economic self-reliance based on 'a proper balance between agriculture and other essential industries'. They differed only in emphasis from the seven aims which, to this day, appear in the Coru, the party's book of rules.

Lemass wanted the organisation called the Republican Party, but de Valera's view prevailed. Fianna Fáil, he argued, suggested continuity. It was a title sometimes given to the Irish Volunteers, who had split from Redmond's National Volunteers in 1913 and, after the Rising, were to form the core of the Irish Republican Army. The Volunteers bore — and the Free State Army kept — the 'F.F.' insignia on their caps. An old comrade from the Volunteers, the O'Rahilly, and the writer, the tAthair Peadar Ó Laoghaire, had been consulted and had approved the name. As far as de Valera was concerned, the title had two other merits: it echoed the Golden Age and, as he wryly observed, it was nearly impossible to translate. Fianna Fáil, sometimes rendered the Soldiers of Destiny, took the attentive nationalist back to the Fianna, the legendary warriors of Fionn Mac Cumhail. To de Valera, as to many a nationalist leader elsewhere, it was necessary

11

to forge such links with a mythical past, when heroic deeds were done and sung, and unity was never questioned. In Dev's eyes, along with the simple aims he had set for Fianna Fáil, these tableaux of the past formed a compelling vision of the future. He did not see how anyone could fail to be attracted to it. Lemass who, even then, was less enamoured of such inspirational images, had to make do with the Republican Party in parentheses.

As for coming to terms with existing conditions — meaning the Free State and its institutions, which the majority of the people had already accepted — there was still the argument about the oath, the agonising about the Republic; but the foundations of the party had been laid a month before the famous gathering at the La Scala Theatre, within earshot of the General Post Office in Dublin, on 16 May 1926. I wrote earlier of the organisers' determination to get the party on the road. That was literally what they did: in a Baby Austin car, on bicycles and on foot, they travelled the country, both before and after the inaugural meeting, constantly arguing the case for their New Departure, this time to be the final push for Ireland's freedom. They were like people raking the embers of a dying fire, for they found, in Dev's own words, that 'the hardest thing to fight against was the weariness and apathy [caused by] the long struggle and the miserable economic conditions of the country.' The recruits on whom they depended most were their old comrades of the IRA. Those who had not already given up the struggle and emigrated to America or Australia; war-weary veterans of whom Seán O'Faolain has left a vivid and painful portrait:

These febrile, fractious, bitter, hungry-eyed ex-freedom-fighters were now in every sense out of a job; shabbily dressed, wearing old hats that one liked to think had once been grazed by bullets, their ankle-length overcoats stuffed with manifestos and pamphlets, their mouths thin with enmity and resolve, and one guessed at empty pockets, perhaps even empty stomachs, and wondered how or on what, in God's name, they and theirs lived.

They were drawn to the La Scala, perhaps by the prospect of 'the final push,' shocked maybe by the government's recent ratification of partition, or convinced by the organisers' last resort: the argument that men who hadn't had hand, act or part in the War of Independence were now enjoying the fruits of their sacrifice. With the veterans came the supporters of Gaelic games and the speakers of Gaelic, the teachers, small farmers and farm labourers, many of them, de Valera remarked, from the poorest sections of the community. In his account of the meeting, Kevin Boland does not dwell on any rage or bitterness the audience may have felt. Instead he describes them, defiant and rapturous to the point of delirium:

> They didn't just leave the La Scala. The marched out, heads held high, humming snatches of Civil War songs, back on course to the Republic clearly charted by President de Valera. . . . With their feet firmly planted on the road to being 'A nation once again', they scattered to the four corners of the twenty-six counties, the Free State, to light the flame in their own parishes and pave the way for the writing of Emmet's epitaph.

What provoked this response was not a full-blooded battle-cry but a speech that had few rhetorical flourishes and relied on a simple device to make its point. It asked the audience to put themselves in the position of a young man arriving at the moment of decision: how best to serve the national cause? The context was clear. De Valera declared himself a republican, 'not because of any doctrinaire attachment to any special form of government, but because, in the conditions of Ireland, independence and the Republic must be in practice one and the same thing.' And the young man of strong nationalist feelings was 'without set prejudices or any commitments of

13

his past to hamper him.' Freed of doctrinaire attachment and the hampering commitments of the past, the very handcuffs that had bound Sinn Féin, the young man could examine the existing conditions – the government's betrayal of the Republic and the impotence of republicans in the face of this betrayal – and reach a conclusion. 'He could see that by isolating the oath for attack, the whole situation and England's ultimate control would be exposed.' The oath was the thing. Once it had been abolished, the republicans could take their seats in the Dáil, win control of the Free State and, one by one, the bonds of foreign interference would be cut. As for partition, 'with a united sovereign twenty-six counties, the position would be reached in which the solution of the problem of successfully bringing in the North could be confidently undertaken.' It was, though no-one dared to say so, de Valera's version of Michael Collins's step-by-step approach to the national question, which the republicans had already rejected.

With the establishment of the party, the first step had been taken. By focusing attention on the oath, de Valera had avoided discussion on more difficult questions, such as the nature of the Republic. The audience at the La Scala had heard what they wanted to hear and were swayed by what they believed to be his intentions as much as by what he said. The purists could argue to their hearts' content. Though the party faithful would always have a place in their hearts for them, the party itself would not be bound by their theology. Fianna Fáil had been given its article of faith and there was, once more, a job to be done. For the organisers, it meant a return to the towns and villages, mountainy parishes and lonely roads, wherever anyone could be found to listen and to take on the task of organisation. It took three visits to Seán Moylan, one of Cork's most powerful IRA leaders, before Gerry Boland could convince him that he should join. In Kerry, Austin Stack refused to be converted. During one tour of West Cork, de Valera and Mullins travelled 1,700

14

miles and set up 45 cumainn, Mullins carrying out repairs on their car while Dev thought out the next line of attack. In Ennis, he told his constituents: 'I stand for the Irish Republic, for the full freedom of Ireland, as thoroughly today as I stood nine years ago when I first came before you.' It was a necessary reassurance because objections to the New Departure had been raised. 'If we do not recognise the facts, we cannot make progress. For the moment we have been driven out of the citadel and I am asking our people to attack it again and retake it. I cannot rally the people to a fresh attack if I keep on shouting that I have got the citadel already.' And there was not a square yard of the country where it could be said: 'Here the Republic exists and no foreign force can drive us out of it.'

Many other painful facts had to be faced before Fianna Fáil deputies finally took their seats in the Dáil in August 1927; and none was more painful than the continued existence of the oath when they did so. At the party's first ardfheis, de Valera had warned the government that if the path of peaceful progress and national evolution was barred, 'then the road of revolution will beckon and will be taken.' But after the 1927 election the path to the Dáil chamber was, indeed, blocked when the party's members tried to enter. They decided to embark not on a revolutionary course but on legal proceedings against their exclusion. One of the means they chose was to have a petition signed by 75,000 voters calling for a constitutional referendum. Then, in July 1927, Kevin O'Higgins, the vice-president, was murdered and the government reacted by introducing three stern measures to protect the State. The first was a Public Safety Bill, the second an electoral amendment designed to put an end to abstention and the third a Bill abolishing the provision for the initiation of petitions leading to constitutional change. De Valera condemned the murder of O'Higgins as a crime that cut at the root of representative government, but in its aftermath he felt more strongly than ever that 'all doors were being closed [by the government] on constitutional actions by Fianna Fáil, all except one — that into Leinster House across which lay the barrier of the oath.'

Throughout the summer, he worried the question endlessly and by early August he was confiding to friends: 'The Fianna Fáil way of removing the oath from outside is being made definitely impossible and will, I expect, have to be abandoned.' It was abandoned but not before, in a manoeuvre of Byzantine complexity, he had produced the formula of the empty formula:

> It has . . . been repeatedly stated, and it is not uncommonly believed, that the required declaration is not an oath; that the signing of it implies no contractual obligation, and that it has no binding significance in conscience or in law, that, in short, it is merely an empty formula which deputies could conscientiously sign without becoming involved, or involving their nation, in obligations of loyalty to the English Crown.

De Valera recognised all too clearly what an opportunity he was handing to his enemies, what a contradiction to his friends. The oath, after all, had been the central issue, if not the sole cause, of the Treaty split and the Civil War. The Republicans had campaigned assiduously — on the last occasion in the June election — for its abolition. It had been a crucial argument for the establishment of Fianna Fáil. He acknowledged the contradiction: 'I grant that what we did was contrary to all our former actions, and to everything we stood for — contrary to our declared policy, and to the explicit pledges we gave at the time of our election. It was a step painful and humiliating for us who had to take it and for those who had supported us.'

But the alternative, as he saw it, was Civil War. (Again the echo: Lloyd George had threatened immediate and terrible war.) So he went to Leinster House, removed the Bible to a far corner of the room, covered the oath in the register with some papers and signed. 'I am not taking any oath,' he said, 'or giving any promise of faithfulness to the King of England or to any power outside the people of Ireland. I am putting my name here merely as a formality to get the permission necessary to enter amongst the other Teachtaí that were elected by the people of Ireland, and I want you to know that no other meaning is to be attached to what I am doing.' It was a lame excuse and he knew it, but despite the triumphant shout which he expected 'from every British propagandist and every enemy of Irish independence' hailing 'this token of our submission' it was a way out of a cruel dilemma. The most favourable view of this solution was that it had rescued the republican movement from prolonged impotence. But whatever its logical contradictions, it marked a great turning point in the history of parliamentary government in Ireland and made certain that parliamentary democracy would prevail.

The character of the party had already been formed — republican but not doctrinaire, claiming continuity but avoiding commitment to the past, accepting the framework of the State but pledged to change it, fundamentally if possible. To its opponents it was elusive, its leader a Houdini, and secretive in a tradition that went back to the Fenians and beyond. As he himself said later, de Valera kept many of its policies under his hat. Compared with the Cumann na nGaedheal government, it was radical, though its own spokesmen sometimes went to considerable lengths to demonstrate that it was not. Seán T. O'Kelly, in particular, declared that it was as Catholic, indeed more Catholic, than any other political group. The fact that many of its leading members had been excommunicated did nothing to diminish the certainty with which the claim was made. Excommunication was somewhat like the oath — you could take it or leave it. The bishops issued condemnations of the party's radicalism — there were hints at communism and threats to private property. Lemass's famous description, a slightly constitutional party, could be adduced in evidence: the bishops had identified themselves

17

with the Free State and its government. A party set on changing one by dispossessing the other was necessarily suspect and obviously dangerous. De Valera's appeal for unity among all sections of nationalist opinion could be dismissed as rhetoric. Besides, he appeared to be more concerned with the physical force men than with those who had already embarked on a constitutional career. Given the nature of his party, it was hardly surprising: some of its key men were still, in a sense, on the run. To them, at least, his threat of revolution, if the path of evolution were blocked, was real enough. Not only was he trying to win back old friends in Sinn Féin; among the converts he had made were those who were still doubtful about constitutional methods. The pike was in the thatch; Dev had only to say the word and it would be taken down. The 1932 election proved a point for the critics who claimed ambivalence; the IRA lent a hand, as canvassers and as self-appointed guardians of the party's meetings, in some areas extending this role to break up the meetings of its opponents. After the election and the dismissal of Eoin O'Duffy, the Garda Commissioner, the IRA's role in the 1932 campaign was to be used partly to justify the formation of the Blueshirts and the mounting of another, arguably more serious threat to constitutional politics. But in 1932 Fianna Fáil emerged as the largest party in the Dáil, a position from which it has never been dislodged. And, though it had to rely in the beginning on Labour's support to form a government, it was to hold power for almost 40 of the next 54 years.

At first, the party set about delivering de Valera's promises, a mixed blessing since that meant fighting an economic war with Britain as well as dismantling much of the old imperial apparatus. It was possible, in a heady patriotic mood, to link the two, as it was possible to see the economic war as part of a bigger campaign to make the country self-sufficient; the other part was the operation of protectionist policy designed to encourage native industry. The idea was that progress towards political and economic independence should go hand in hand. Thus, the withholding of land annuities, which gave rise to the economic war, could be seen as an advance running parallel with the abolition of the oath. National pride, stiffened by the political campaign, would ensure that the poorer farmers, who bore the brunt of Britain's retaliation for loss of the annuities, were not overwhelmed by the devaluation of their stock, compulsory tillage and rock-bottom prices. In due course, the political campaign led to the abolition of the oath and the office of Governor-General; the enactment of a new constitution, negotiation of a new Anglo-Irish Agreement and the declaration of neutrality. De Valera's biographers could argue: 'After the Agreement of 1938 and six years of neutrality in the war, it was manifest to all that total independence for the twenty-six counties had been secured.' On the political front, the claim was well founded, but that was as far as it went. For, though most Irish commentators were to agree that neutrality was a defiant, probably necessary assertion of independence, none could maintain that the attempt to win economic independence had succeeded or that the party emerged unscathed in 1948 from its first sixteen years in office. Protection of native industry failed to produce self-sufficiency; the struggle over the land annuities virtually ruined many small farmers. And the party which had begun with a radical reputation was seen instead to have fulfilled Seán T. O'Kelly's Catholic promise, ensuring stricter censorship, prohibitions on divorce and contraception, and acknowledgment of the special position of the Catholic Church. This, however, received little attention inside the party and, outside it, was noted only by such writers as O'Faolain, Frank O'Connor, Liam O'Flaherty and Peadar O'Donnell, critics whom the party either did not hear or felt it could afford to ignore. Its slogan in the 1948 Election was 'Play Safe.'

The reason the party fumbled and lost that election had little to do with its economic failures or its restrictive social

19

legislation. Its temporary loss of nerve was caused by the emergence of Clann na Poblachta, a party which, in many respects, resembled Fianna Fáil itself with its republican and radical appeal tempting all classes and geographical regions. In government, Clann na Poblachta's considerable influence on the decision to declare a Republic was a further cause for alarm and when government and party disintegrated over the Mother and Child Scheme in 1951 Fianna Fáil was relieved by the sight of so much political wreckage.

The party's reaction to the humiliation of a potential challenger was smug and cynical; it ignored the damage which the affair inflicted on the South and the opportunity for claims of Rome rule which it presented to the Unionists.

Did it shatter the faith of the party's supporters? It did not. The 1957 election, de Valera's last as leader, was a triumph. It saw the 'old team' back in office with 79 seats in the Dáil, its most substantial majority to date; but de Valera was, at last, contemplating retirement. The leadership passed quietly to Lemass and the party quite dramatically changed course. From Lemass's arrival in office, in 1959, until the outbreak of violence in the North ten years later, it was to concentrate on industrial development and free trade, on easing Anglo-Irish relations and a gradualist approach to partition, on consolidating and risking the independence that had been achieved. Industrial development had been promoted under de Valera's leadership, but with the emphasis on protection; economic planning had been proposed by the second Inter-Party government but had not been implemented by the time it left office. The impression of decades of neglect which characterised the late 'fifties was not altogether accurate, but it was clear that the old policies had been inadequate and there was a need for adventurous action. Lemass took it, in partnership with a senior civil servant, Ken Whitaker, and he encouraged his ministers to do the same.

The First Programme for Economic Expansion was itself an admission that protectionist policies had failed. Lemass's meetings with the Prime Minister of Northern Ireland, Terence O'Neill, underlined the failure of their predecessors even to nod in each other's direction. Surprisingly, there were few public complaints at either of these changes; and had anyone complained loudly and persistently it is doubtful if they would have been granted more than an impatient hearing. The bleak years of emigration and the frozen immobility of partitioned minds reproached potential critics before they began. What was missing was any substantial debate about the future of a society now being shaped by influences more pervasive than occupying forces or alien administrations. A party which had thought purely in terms of occupation and administration, which was now engaged in the long-delayed full-time business of providing for its people, was poorly equipped to meet the challenge. It was enough that jobs were being provided, increasingly by foreign companies, that living standards were being improved, that schools were being built, more children being educated and, with welfare services expanding, fewer people, young or old, falling victim to poverty. It was enough to satisfy an electorate now enjoying increased mobility, their own and foreign television services, relaxed censorship, bigger cars, brighter homes and a sense of optimism which accommodated some questioning of the past. Not everyone was satisfied: the farmers objected volubly to what they saw as a shift to urban politics with consequent neglect of their interests. They marched on cities and towns to demand restoration of their rights. There were demonstrations, too, against the government's encouragement of building speculators at the expense of Dublin's poor and of the city's architecture. The 50th anniversary of 1916 provoked comparisons between the promise of the Proclamation and the achievements of the intervening years. Looking about them, some people asked: 'Was it for this the Wild Geese spread the grey wing upon every tide?' And the answer came back from the men in the mohair suits: 'Does it matter? We've come into our own.'

21

The party's first contest for leadership followed these lines. Lemass's decision to retire came suddenly, because of a suspected illness. It took the party by surprise. Unlike de Valera's departure when Lemass's right of succession was undisputed, the leadership was open to competition. Jack Lynch's claim was strong, on the ground of continuity and service. He was Lemass's deputy and the most experienced of the second generation of Ministers. His skill and determination as hurler and footballer had combined with a diffident air and fierce local pride to make him something of a folk hero in Cork city. But the very ordinariness that proved so popular in Cork was seen by many of his parliamentary colleagues as weakness; and the fact that he had no family links with the party or the struggle for independence was considered a disadvantage by those who believed that republicanism was bred in the bone. Lynch was eventually chosen, with the blessings of most of the party's senior members and the support of the vast majority of his colleagues.

The choice, however, was preceded by a test of strength between two other challengers, Charles Haughey and George Colley, contemporaries, old rivals and near neighbours from the north side of Dublin. Their rivalry was to develop into a life-long enmity which, much later, was to sap the energies of the governments they served in, taking the party to the verge of permanent division. In 1966, Haughey, with his close connections in the business world, was seen as the leading representative of the men in the mohair suits, whose flamboyant lifestyle and social ambitions he so obviously shared. Colley was the clean-cut Irish-speaking bearer of an older tradition — concerned, he was to say, lest low standards in high places damage Irish life. Lemass, who was Haughey's father-in-law, refused to be drawn into the conflict. De Valera was beyond the range of active politics in the Presidency. But some survivors from the 'old team' were worried by what they recognised as the incipient dangers of overweening ambition among young Turks who regarded Lynch dismissively as a compromise leader, a caretaker who would look after local affairs while the ground was prepared for the real leadership contest. In fact, Lynch was to lead the party for 13 years during which he was forced to show the steel and resilience his critics believed he had not got. The irony was that no-one who had seen him play Gaelic games at the most demanding level could have doubted his nerve and courage, but that was something his opponents seemed to have ignored. Lynch dismissed Haughey, who was his Minister for Finance, along with Neil Blaney, who was Minister for Agriculture, in May 1970, on suspicion that they had been involved in a conspiracy to import arms. They were acquitted by the courts. Few thought that Lynch and his government could survive the dismissal or the acquittal. The party seemed in imminent danger of being torn apart: Kevin Boland and Micheal Ó Morain, close cabinet colleagues of Haughey and Blaney, chose to resign. Boland set up a new party which failed to win support; Ó Morain lost his Dáil seat; Blaney was eventually forced out of Fianna Fáil but remained, as Boland said, in external association with it; Haughey stayed in the party and recovered, with remarkable speed, a position of influence. Five years after he had stood in the dock, he was again a member of the front bench, serving with men who had accused him and whose resignations he had called for at the moment of his acquittal. By 1977 he was once more a Minister and, by the end of 1979, leader of the party and Taoiseach.

What had set this extraordinary series of events in train was the outbreak of violence in the North in August 1969, only months after Lynch had had a spectacular success in a general election that focused principally on southern issues, such as land speculation and the Labour Party's putatively socialist policies. For over a year, the Northern Ireland Civil Rights Association and Unionist reaction to its claims and activities had been drawing international attention towards Northern Ireland. But not the attention of the government in

Dublin. Southern leaders had long since ceased to regard the North as a live political issue, even during elections. Lemass had dropped the conventional rhetoric on the subject, though he could argue that by making the Republic a more attractive place to live in he was doing as much as de Valera had done to encourage unity; the same could be said of the North-South co-operation that had begun to develop after his meetings with O'Neill. Lynch was following this practical course when the violence started and, within a week, set the ghosts of fifty years on the march. To old questions, about the nature of the State and the party's reason for existence, were added an immediate challenge: whether or not the government was prepared to take military action, in defence of the Catholics of the North (our people) and in line with its constitutional claim to 'the national territory' (our fourth green field).

The cabinet, about whose detailed deliberations we can only speculate, discussed sending the Army into Derry or Newry or both, if not to hold these towns, then to create an international incident which would call for United Nations intervention. Some Ministers argued that, even if action were not to be taken by the State, the government should encourage — and should certainly not discourage — action by the (Catholic) citizens' defence committees or the IRA. Delegations arriving in Dublin were clamouring for help: some specifically asked for guns. Lynch agreed to send field hospitals to the Border and to provide weapons training for Northerners joining the Republic's defence forces. Otherwise, as Conor Cruise O'Brien wrote afterwards, the Taoiseach confined himself to talking like a republican and acting like a pragmatist. Almost a year later, when the Dáil debated the dismissal of Haughey and Blaney in a session that continued day and night for 37½ hours, all that was clear and undisputed was that the crisis had provoked the starkest division of nationalist opinion since the Treaty. Cruise O'Brien, who was then a member of Labour's front bench, looked across the chamber to the uneasy ranks of Fianna Fáil, and ominously summarised the arguments of the opposition: 'The party is sick with a dangerous and infectious sickness. It is incubating the germs of a possible civil war.' Not since de Valera had justified taking the oath and entering the Dáil had the party been called upon to 'face the facts' in such grave and threatening circumstances as when Lynch asked for a vote of confidence in his government, on 9 May 1970. The facts were that, however intense might be the feelings of people in the Republic, the action that many of them wanted would have led to more bloodshed in the North and to instability in the South; that an election precipitated by a Dáil defeat would be fraught with risks of violence that had been absent since the 1930s, and that, win or lose, the party would be divided and damaged beyond repair. The government was given the vote of confidence; in the opinion of its critics, the day of reckoning had merely been postponed, but as Lynch's followers recovered their equilibrium it became clear that it was to be a long postponement.

The party's survival bewildered its opponents and amazed its friends. Not only did Lynch's beleaguered government hold out for two and a half years after the arms crisis, it managed to negotiate Irish membership of the European Economic Community and to bring Anglo-Irish relations to the point where, albeit nine months after its departure, agreement on a power-sharing executive in the North proved possible. It survived the shocks of internment and Bloody Sunday when the British Army shot dead thirteen young men who were taking part in a civil rights march in Derry. Clearly, both the party and public opinion had undergone a change as fundamental as that which marked the emergence of an urban industrial society in the 1960s. The 1977 election, in which Fianna Fáil won a historic victory on policies that appealed primarily to the self-interest of consumers, was the most striking reflection of the new mood. Questions about who did what and why in 1969-'70 were submerged in the excitement of a bargain-basement manifesto, which included proposals to remove rates from houses and tax from cars. The unpopularity of a Coalition of Fine Gael and Labour, which had struggled unsuccessfully against the ebb-tide of recession while giving the impression that it cared little for national pride or civil rights, greatly helped an opposition that promised a return to prosperity, with jobs for all and a standard of living such as the Republic had never enjoyed, at the cost only of wage restraint and a pledge to buy Irish goods.

The country paid dearly for the promises, and Lynch paid the political price for the popularity they had helped to provide. His government's failures were not as dramatic as those of other administrations but, in the wake of so much optimism, a combination of public service strikes, petrol shortages and the private sector's inability or refusal to create employment, proved disastrous: two years after its historic victory, the party suffered bruising defeats in European and local elections. Worse still, from Lynch's point of view, it turned in a feeble performance in two by-elections in Cork city and county. The electoral decline was accompanied by a sustained internal campaign against Lynch himself which caused him to resign, as leader and Taoiseach, somewhat earlier than he had intended. He was prompted to go by friends who believed that a quick decision would ensure Colley's succession. They miscalculated. Haughey was well prepared and won the contest, which was even more bitterly fought than the 1966 rehearsal, by half-a-dozen votes. It took more than three years, however, before he was able to claim undisputed control of the party and then only after Colley's death, the isolation of one of Colley's allies, Martin O'Donoghue, and the expulsion of another, Des O'Malley. Among the conventions which had bound party members for more than fifty years was the untouchable nature of the leadership. It was an essential feature of all populist movements. The campaign against Lynch removed that protection, in the eyes of Colley, O'Malley and O'Donoghue. Colley for-

26

mally announced, soon after Haughey's election, that the rule of loyalty no longer applied; it was the signal marking the start of an unprecedented campaign against the new leader. Between 1981 and 1983, his position was challenged on three occasions and, though the challenges were unsuccessful, the party suffered a period of turbulence unlike any that Fianna Fáil — or any other nationalist party — had endured since the crisis of 1970 had set its factions at each other's throats.

3

A Certain View

To begin with it was, as all populist movements are, its leader's party. Though Lemass was its architect and the 'old team' its faithful engineers, de Valera gave it its tone. Fianna Fáil spoke with his slow, country accent as he spoke to us when, like an elderly relative coming to look us over, he visited Clare. Standing at the door of the train, he was taller than a missioner on the altar and, with his long, dark cloak and distant gaze, twice as solemn. He seemed to look beyond the crowd on the gravelled platform towards the guard of honour with its shouldered guns and peaked caps turned backwards and beyond them to the younger men who had marched before the train with blazing turf-sods on bobbing forks. Looking out above their heads to where our low hills crouched in the darkness, he slowly said: 'Muintir Chreatlaigh' — and the whole parish let out a yell of delight and recognition such as no missioner was every likely to hear, for this man had been theirs for close on three decades; he was at the height of his power and he was part of their history, like the flying columns on the hills all those years ago. He thanked them for coming out to welcome him, told them how pleased he was to be among them, reminded them that once again he was looking for their support. The reminder was hardly necessary: it was thrown in almost as an afterthought, but the train was half-way to Ballycar by the time the cheering stopped; and he must have been well in bed in Carmody's Hotel in Ennis before the men at the crossroads turned to go home. Their talk was not of policies or oaths or the rights and wrongs of taking seats in the Dáil. It was of the chief himself and how he looked, for they were secure in that certain view of the world, the particular and unmistakable view which the party shared with no other institution, human or divine.

What Fianna Fáil stood for could be summarised in two words: the Republic. Summarised but not explained; de Valera simply defined it as being synonymous with independence, to be achieved by unity, self-sufficiency and the restoration of Irish. In the past fifty years, neutrality had been added, but that's a conditional policy: no one, from de Valera to Haughey, has been prepared to exclude the possibility that it might be changed. Apart from its being united, self-sufficient, Irish-speaking and, at least temporarily, neutral, the nature of the Republic has not been discussed, let alone described in detail.

What the party was against was, from the beginning, a good deal clearer, though with some qualifications. A Sinn Féin man was asked during the War of Independence what his party's title meant. His answer was simple: 'Vingeance, bejasus.' Fianna Fáil belonged for years to the 'vingeance, bejasus' school of nationalism — and showed signs of returning to it in the 'eighties. It was anti-British, or more anti-British than its opponents whom it considered pro-British if only because they disagreed with Fianna Fáil. It was anti-Treaty, though that was a distinction which diminished as the trappings of association with Britain were removed, and it disappeared altogether when an Inter-Party government declared the State a Republic. It was anti-partition, its strongest rhetorical suit even if, from time to time, there was nothing to choose between its rhetoric and that of the opposition. It was anti-Free State, to the extent that, even in government, it gave the impression of disapproving of the twenty-six county regime, managing to sound as if it were still impatient to take office. With its country air, it maintained a suspicion of towns and cities, disliked anything that savoured of modern life and had no time or place for

29

intellectuals other than de Valera himself. It regarded the Irish language and Gaelic games, like the past, as its private property and the national question as the issue on which everyone was finally to be judged. Someone who was sound on the national question could safely be described as 'one of our own', although here, too, there were problems of definition. If the Church, the Party and the Games were the pillars of Irish society — and you did not have to ask which church, which party or which games — it did not always follow that they leaned in the same direction. There was a period during which the party revelled in an anti-clerical reputation. In the elections of 1932 and 1933, the bishops detected what they thought were threats of communism, opposition to their authority and an ambivalent attitude to force. Micheál Ó hAodha, who was growing up in Clare at the time, heard Michael Fogarty, 'Black Mick', the bishop of Killaloe, fulminate against the antichrist de Valera who was about to arrive in Ennis.

Down through the years your kith and kin have stood side by side with your bishops in the struggle for faith and fatherland. But I cannot gloss over the regrettable fact that in more recent times there has been an unfortunate tendency on the part of the more impressionable, perhaps I should say, immature among you to be swayed by catch-cries and slogans, rather than to accept the guidance of your pastors. The outcome of such confused thinking is that some misguided individuals have turned their backs on those who stand firmly for the maintenance of law and order in public life, and have given their unthinking support to those who would substitute for the ballot-box, the petrol-can and the bullet. I need hardly remind you of the dire consequences which followed on such anarchy in our recent and tragic past. It was perfidy of this kind that resulted in the deaths of President Griffith and General Collins. Arthur Griffith

30

died of a broken heart, and I need not recall for you the horror of Michael Collins's end. Never, never, did the Woman of the Piercing Wail cry so bitterly as that day at Beal na Blath.

No one could doubt what he had in mind: 'His tones seemed to echo in the Gothic crevices of the Pro-Cathedral. Even the punters outside had to hand it to him that it was a powerful sermon which confirmed what they already knew, that it was hardly likely that St Flannan or the bishop would vote for de Valera.' As for the politician:

> Compared to Black Mick he is no orator. He goes on and on about the Republic — the Republic — the Republic — but the crowd listens in hushed awe. He stirs some chord and there is a ringing in their ears as he talks about an ancient wrong in a new way. Although it was fifteen years since he came to Clare, he was still a stranger, a Spaniard, a rugby player from Rockwell. But he could talk to them in their own language: the voice was not that of the Bronx or of Booterstown but of Bruree, Croom and Bruff, and of the rich Co. Limerick farmers who took their holidays in Lisdoonvarna. . . . He strung placenames like beads on a rosary of rememberance; and the men of Tulla, Bodyke and Corofin cheered wildly, madly at every mention of their parish . . . It was not the promises he gave, for he gave few, but it was his indignation at their lot that moved them in the dark recesses of their souls.

The party, living up to the few promises, introduced a quixotic programme of land distribution, cleared some of the worst urban slums in Western Europe, expanded and improved the welfare system and encouraged the development of Irish industries, thus justifying the support it had had from small farmers and workers during its first decade in office. It was a decade in which the promise of radicalism seemed likely to

31

be fulfilled and the contrast with Cumann na nGaedheal and their immediate successors in Fine Gael was most sharply drawn. But what Seán O'Faolain called 'that restless ghost, our past' refused to go away. The old injustice — of the Treaty, the Civil War and partition — was more deeply embedded in the minds of the party's idealists than any concern with social wrongs that were, if not older, certain to last longer.

> Always at their backs they had the loving and inspiring memories of their dead comrades; always before them there shone the light of the promised land, the day when they would once more proclaim the living Republic and undo all the harm that had been done to the national faith by their faithless fellows. In those harsh years the iron entered into the souls of our nationalist left. During forty years it never melted. It was too useful a lode, if only to stiffen their resolve to prove to their countrymen that they, who had been so often mocked as hair-splitters, dreamers and extremists, could, in power, manage Ireland's affairs as well or better than their traitorous predecessors.
>
> Did they? They did. Just as well, sometimes better, and in exactly the same manner; partly because the way of life of 'the merchants and the commercial interests' was by now too well entrenched to be uprooted easily; partly because once in power they became cagey; but mainly because their blazing mystique still had no social content.

It was, however, their blazing mystique — de Valera's cry of indignation — which sustained the party's members and did much to attract and hold the support of more than 40 per cent, sometimes over half, of the electorate down the years. It continued to sway the voters even after Fianna Fáil had settled into the habits of power and there was nothing to choose between its policies and personnel and those of 'their faithless fellows', nothing to distinguish the supporters of one party from those of the other except, perhaps, that certain view of the past which stretched beyond their more recent struggles to O'Donovan Rossa and the Fenians and, beyond them, through generations of fierce and futile resistance, to Fionn Mac Cumhail and the Red Branch Knights. The party, in its title, laid claim to this past and some of its more romantic members spoke as though Brian Boru had been a cumann chairman in Kincora or Cuchulain one of their separated brethren in the North. 'It is hard to be calm', de Valera said on hearing of the boundary agreement in 1925, 'when one remembers that it is our fairest province that is being cut off. The Ulster that the Irishman of every province loves best next to his own. The Ulster of Cuchulain, the Ulster of the Red Branch Knights. The Ulster of the O'Neills and the O'Donnells. The Ulster in whose sacred sod rest the bones of Patrick, Columcille and Brian of the Tributes.'

In prison a few years earlier, Seán MacEntee had discovered that de Valera knew little of 'our fairest province' that every Irishman 'loved best next to his own'. MacEntee, who was from Belfast, was surprised and irritated; but generations of party faithful — and generations of schoolchildren — were to hear more of the Red Branch Knights than they heard of the Orange Order or the Ulster Volunteer Force until the guns and drums of the 'sixties sounded dangerously close.

Nationalist movements invariably reach into the past, either to prove their own authenticity or to provide inspiration for their members and supporters, especially when, with the immediate task completed and the colonial administration overthrown, the nationalist leaders see their new regimes in danger of appearing less radical or less exciting than the struggle had promised. Traditional religious values, too, are relied on to meet the need for continuity. In Fianna Fáil, loyalty to a real or mythical past and to traditional religious values was taken for granted, as Tod Andrews makes plain in his lively and sinewy volumes of autobiography. Andrews, who was one of the party but not in it, writes of his own feelings: 'I was in thrall to Pearse; to the standards of Cuchulain and Finn. I thought all the leaders of the Movement were equally in thrall to these standards.' Of Liam Lynch, the chief of staff of the IRA, who was killed near the end of the Civil War, he says: 'He was a good man, brave, strong-willed, uncomplicated to the point of simplicity . . . He had the religious faith of an Irish countryman. God and the saints were real to him. He regarded them as allies of the Irish Republic to which he had dedicated his life.' And he recalls meeting, during the takeover of RIC barracks in Cork, a man called Seán McCarthy who was 'typical of many of the older people' in the Republican Movement: 'To him the Movement was a combination of the Gaelic League, the GAA, the IRA and the Catholic Church. He shared what was a commonly held opinion at the time that unless you were a Catholic and a member of the GAA you could not be a good Irishman.' McCarthy, as if to prove the point, became a Fianna Fáil TD, Lord Mayor of Cork and President of the GAA.

None of this means that either the republican movement or the party was conservative through and through. Liam Mellowes, whose portrait still hangs in the party's headquarters, had become a convinced socialist, if not a Marxist, by the time of his execution during the Civil War. He was one of the martyrs called in aid by Lynch's critics in the early 'seventies. De Valera quoted James Connolly in his inaugural address to the party and, forty years on, smilingly acknowledged that it had had a definite socialist flavour. But there was irony in the passage that he chose — 'Ireland, as distinct from her people, is nothing to me' — not because of any indifference to wrong and suffering but because of the number of Irish people who left Ireland during his years in government. And Peadar O'Donnell searched in vain for converts to Marxism. Andrews explains: 'The "class war" about

34

which Peadar spoke so convincingly would have been un-known — even as a phrase — to almost everyone in the Move-ment. In our estimation there were only two classes. There were the British with their dependents and hangers-on of whom the most objectionable group was the Castle Catholics, and there were the Irish. There was no Marxian slide rule appropriate to Irish social conditions.'

It was, in the party's early days, a case of the old struggle conducted in new circumstances. Time and again, de Valera, Boland, Andrews and others speak of the Irish when they mean Fianna Fáil and of the British, the imperialists and their dependents when they mean Cumann na nGaedheal or Fine Gael. The legacy survives: in the 'seventies and 'eighties, not only were critical outsiders described as anti-national; the epithet was applied by Haughey's supporters to the internal critics of his leadership. The assumption was implicit (occasionally made explicit) that anyone who opposed the party line was acting on behalf of the British establishment or one of its more sinister agencies. John M. Feehan's *Operation Brogue* is dedicated to the proposition that politicians inside and outside the party, and journalists inside and outside the country were engaged, in the early 'eighties, in a conspiracy to undermine the Fianna Fáil leader: 'The demarcation lines between the activities of the British Secret Service, Fine Gael and sections of Fianna Fáil were very difficult to chart. I did not find any concrete evidence that they worked as a co-ordinated unit together. Rather I would say they moved on parallel lines having the same end result in view. . . .' It was a new and not very convincing twist to old suspicions.

The party itself had long been suspect in the eyes of its constitutional opponents, partly because of the blazing mystique of which O'Faolain wrote, the quasi-military and secretive nature of its organisation and sporadic outbursts of republican militancy, reflecting overt support for the IRA, by some of its members. Far from denying them, the party cherished its nationalist antecedents, constitutional or paramilitary — sometimes, it seemed, the bloodier the better. There were the obvious lines of descent: from the United Irishmen, who were the first militant separatists, through O'Connell's campaign for Catholic Emancipation and the Repeal movement to the Young Irelanders, the Fenians and the Land League; from the IRB, the Volunteers and the IRA to Sinn Féin. There were less obvious lines, from the Ribbonmen and faction fighters of the pre-Famine days, whose legacy was the violence of agrarian struggle and, in some parts of the country, of sectarian feuds. There had been times when constitutional and paramilitary campaigns went hand-in-hand or, at least, appeared to complement each other. Even where the connections were illusory, they had an effect. If Parnell's condemnations of force were sometimes taken by his supporters as evidence that he really believed in it, then de Valera's position was doubly difficult. His participation in the Rising and the Civil War, as well as the statements he'd made in the early years of the party, led some of his followers to the conclusion that he was never really opposed to the IRA even when he was in deadly earnest.

But just as Parnell took advantage of the Phoenix Park murders in 1882 to drive the whole nationalist movement closer to constitutionalism, de Valera used O'Higgins's murder in 1927 and IRA attacks on the gardaí during the 'thirties to reinforce the constitutional basis of Fianna Fáil. He even succeeded, in the 'forties, in introducing military tribunals and mandatory death sentences without any major objections from the party. 'Our policy of patience is over,' he said. 'I warn those now planning new crimes against the nation that they will not be allowed to continue their policy of sabotage. They have set the law at defiance. The law will be enforced against them. If the present law is not sufficient, it will be strengthened; and in the last resort, if no other law will suffice, then the government will invoke the ultimate law — the safety of the people.' The people and the party acquiesced.

The party had grown accustomed to weathering contradictions whether they arose from taking the oath, its relations with the church or punishing the violence on which, it was said, some of its members had an each-way bet. Anti-clerical or not, it could happily call itself Catholic — and list Tone, Emmet and Davis among its forebears. (To tidy things up, they could be given the status of honorary Catholics for the day.) While bishops or priests agreed with the party, its members had no difficulty in accepting their authority. Once they disagreed with or condemned the party, the conclusion was obvious: the bishops were wrong and their authority could safely be set aside, for the time being anyhow. It was a form of mutual excommunication which lasted until the bishops came to their senses. The party, however, adopted a stern line with its own wayward members, dealing quickly and ruthlessly in what would now be classed as Stalinist fashion with almost any show of recalcitrance. 'Almost' — Dan Breen, the Tipperary IRA leader who had taken his seat in the Dáil months before the rest of the republicans in 1927, and Tommy Mullins, who took an independent socialist line and was expelled but readmitted, were remarkable exceptions to the rule which overrode all other considerations: whatever the contradictions or policy changes, and whatever their scruples or logical objections, the members accepted that the party came first. Its discipline, like its secrecy, had a military air. To be disloyal was to be airbrushed out of history, much as mid-European politicians disappeared from party photographs in the 'fifties.

There were, indeed, some respects in which the party and the church resembled each other. It is not too far-fetched to imagine de Valera and the 'old team' as a Pope and his senior Cardinals forever circling the eternal truth that, come what may, their authority was indisputable. There were occasions, of course, when de Valera himself introduced a touch of monastic serge as when, in 1943, he delivered his famous message of frugal comfort, redolent of a rural simplicity that never was and a vision of contentment that could never be. It can be argued that, far from suggesting that we emulate the Plain People of Pennsylvania, with the Amish community of Bruree, he was offering some steadying advice to citizens who were trying to get by on war-time rations, wet turf and Portuguese brandy masquerading as the real thing. It is, indeed, possible that his lifelong emphasis on rural values was an attempt to keep people's expectations in check in a country which could afford few of the luxuries that its neighbours enjoyed, but much more likely that it was a reflection of the party's dependence on rural votes, wedded to a conviction that, socially, politically and psychologically, small units could be more easily managed — and probably suited the Irish temperament better — than big towns and cities. The struggle against the Norman habit of living in towns was as old as the conquest. The party's attachment to the symbols of pre-conquest society served both its immediate purposes and the need it felt to take possession of the past as if it were a private inheritance.

Seán McCarthy of Cork was quite accurate when he counted two other organisations, the Gaelic League and the GAA, with the IRA and the Church, as part of the broader nationalist movement. The GAA, like the party, was rooted in every parish in the country and, like the party, had a distinctly rural air. Its ban on foreign games, and on members of the RIC and the British Army, underlined its Irishness in a way that reflected the influence of the IRB. Though that was not its intention, it also had the effect of excluding Protestants, many of the middle classes and substantial numbers of the urban working class who had played or followed 'foreign games' since their schooldays. How closely related were the games and the party? Close enough for a chance remark by de Valera to have created a bitter public controversy in which he was, as near as dammit, accused of national treachery. All he'd said was that he thought rugby a suitable game for Irish boys. He had played it himself in Rockwell. Organised like the old parish factions, the GAA sometimes gave rise to the same kind of friction but its most lasting contribution to the nationalist movement was the provision of a framework within which local social leaders could operate. At least one historian considered the GAA to be in many ways 'the true parent of the IRA of the Anglo-Irish war of 1919-1921' and Kevin Boland, recounting his father's role in the recruitment of members and organisers to the party, told how 'everywhere [Gerry Boland] went his brother Harry had been before him on work for either the GAA, the IRB, Sinn Féin or the IRA or for all four.' In his view, there was no doubt where GAA men stood: their clubs were called after 'subversives and terrorists like Wolfe Tone, Robert Emmet, Charles Kickham, Thomas Davis and even the ungodly Parnell.' The association had, in fact, been bitterly divided both by the Parnell split and by the IRB's efforts to dominate it. It was to survive one further trauma, brought on by the Civil War, before emerging once more as a major nationalist, but non-partisan, force in the 1920s. During its centenary celebrations in 1984, Jack Lynch — once suspended because of the ban — paid tribute to its role in mobilising non-violent nationalism at a time when leadership and organisational ability were what the movement needed and to the healing qualities of the games in the aftermath of the Civil War. A glance at the membership of Dáil and Senate, certainly in the 'sixties and 'seventies, is sufficient to convince the most sceptical observer that a good record on the hurling or football field became to the aspiring politician of any party what a national record had once been to the members of Fianna Fáil. The medals are fairly evenly distributed on all benches; but, as with the past, the party claims the heart of the organisation as its own.

There is stronger evidence to link the party (again, informally) with the language movement. The Gaelic League in the early years of the century was a forcing ground for nationalist leaders and activists, producing about half of those who served as government ministers or as senior civil servants in the first fifty years after independence. Unlike the GAA, it was not a mass movement, but its influence was at least as widespread. Fear of English culture, particularly as a secular influence, caused some clergy to join — the old joke about puritans, lay and clerical, believing that it was more difficult to express sinful thoughts in Irish had more than a grain of truth in it. Some of them were also convinced that Irish dancing provided fewer occasions of sin than foreign dances; ceilis, in any event, were more likely to be supervised by watchful Leaguers intent on preventing the corruption of Irish youth by some alien influence. Old republicans were attracted to the Gaelic League by its separatist tone and direction, Anglo-Irish intellectuals by the opportunity to make and maintain connections with the nationalist community. Catholic businessmen supported the League's activities as a wholesome antidote to subversive and immoral ideas from outside: the seeds of cultural apartheid were present even in the early days of the League.

The party, with its emphasis on the restoration of the language and the need to promote Irish culture, naturally provided a political home for those who had served an apprenticeship in the League. Tom Garvin, one of the most perceptive and scholarly analysts of modern Irish nationalism, has written that 'the most persistently successful variable in distinguishing Fianna Fáil from most of the other [parties] and, in particular, from Fine Gael, has been a cultural one; it has always been supported disproportionately by Irish speakers.' This is not, and never was, a characteristic confined to Gaeltacht areas, which are too few and far between to make much of an impact on voting patterns. It refers to Irish speakers generally, or even to people whose declared love of the language is in inverse proportion to their ability to speak it. When, after generations of lip service, it became clear that revival was not a particularly popular endeavour, the party still clung to the policy. The language had become a badge of national piety — de Valera eventually placed it higher in his list of priorities than unity — but with every year that passed it seemed less and less likely to be accepted as anything more than a badge, though it was still thought unpatriotic to say so. As far as the party was concerned, it was a badge that served it well.

But in the party's subtle and complex make-up, can any ingredient be identified as the source of its success? None, in isolation, fully explains its attraction for the Irish electorate. Not even the blazing mystique, the iron that entered the old warriors' souls during their years of waiting, could have shaped their destiny if it had not been for the determination to prove that they could manage as well as their treacherous predecessors. And, though they struggled against it for a while, the more they proved their ability the more they came to resemble the predecessors whom they scorned. They became, more clearly as the years went by, a party of the twenty-six county State, living with and occasionally overcoming the limitations of that State, until its people were 'our people' and even the blazing mystique took second place to their interests and protection. The party changed, and was to change again, radically and of necessity, until that certain view of the past was almost submerged by overwhelming demands of generations too young to remember and too harassed to care.

4

Our People

The New Departure was old-fashioned, even for the 'twenties and 'thirties and a state where three-quarters of the population lived outside the cities and towns. Europe was looking hopefully to the left and nervously to the right, searching for signs of a future that would work and coming face to face with the spectre on the Brocken. The party looked neither to left nor right but steadfastly to the past and drew on the spirit of the nation, almost but not quite as Thomas Davis and the Young Irelanders had dreamed of it eighty years before. Even in Lemass's time, when urban matters had become the focus of attention, the party still kept its country air, as if for old time's sake, like someone who had gone to work in the city but could never bring himself to think of it as home.

Kevin Boland caught its mood of defiance when he wrote of the delegates marching from the inaugural meeting chanting songs of the Civil War. They were carrying the message of the Republic, the revival of the spirit of the nation, to the four corners of the Free State and they knew the people for whom their message was intended: men clustered round their creameries or at the open door of a forge on some blustery hillside, eager as of old to hear the word from Dublin. 'Murmurs marched along the valleys, get you ready quick and soon, for the pikes must be together by the Rising of the Moon.' The party's founders were convinced that there was one sense in which these country places had not changed since John Keegan Casey's pikemen sent down the word, though there had been many changes for the worse since the 1840s. The Famine was now etched on the folk memory; new betrayals had been added, with every generation, to the litany of defeat; and with every defeat, as with every crop failure, a new wave of embittered emigrants had left behind them communities that were dispirited and leaderless. There were still those who, against all the odds, and with the vigour of a fresh generation would respond to the cry, 'A Nation Once Again'.

This was the spirit to which de Valera and Fianna Fáil appealed, almost certainly with something akin to desperation beneath the buoyancy and defiance of their rhetoric; for the latest defeat had been too recent and too bitter to be converted, in the alchemy of memory, into some heroic tale. De Valera himself admitted, in a letter to a friendly American editor, the low spirits of the people, the poor plight of the economy and the growing acceptance of the new, truncated state. Besides which, another wave of emigration had begun and threatened to carry off what remained of the force that had been active in the Four Glorious Years (1918 to '22) and the Civil War. And between the zealotry of the IRA and the disillusion of their erstwhile comrades there was a rugged path which led inevitably to compromise and, with no great assurance, to power. All of the 'old team's' considerable persuasive ability and all of de Valera's undeniable gift of leadership would be needed if they were to convince people to take it.

As we have seen, they had on their side the argument that power had fallen into the hands of politicians who had done nothing to earn it, and their determination to prove that they could govern as well or better than their opponents. They were inspired by the blazing mystique and that legacy of the past, their private inheritance, which fitted them — and no one else — for the role of completing the task on which the heroes of of 1916 had embarked. And there was the conviction that the nation and the party were one, wedded, as time and the party progressed, in a phrase that was as simple and evocative as the rest of their programme: our people.

Simple, evocative and subtle, the beauty of it was that it was capable of many meanings, yet — like the blazing mystique and the invocation of the past — it erected an invisible barrier which distinguished the faithful from the rest, a point of reference in a land without maps. In the language of the Golden Age it embraced the 'historic Irish nation', much as Davis had intended; it was quickly redefined to exclude anyone who had supported the Treaty or backed the State's first government. At first it had some, albeit vague, class connotations, in deference to the small farmers, farm labourers and industrial workers who stood their ground against vested interests and begrudgers to make Fianna Fáil the party of the open-necked shirts, as Donogh O'Malley remembered it. When Dev called them 'our people' he knew that they knew what he meant and even if, somewhere along the line, his plans for them went astray, they turned up year after year at ard-fheiseanna, contributed their shillings to party funds and their wisdom to its discussions, and never counted the cost. Another generation, the men in the mohair suits, might have given less time and thought to the party's affairs; they wrote bigger cheques and some, at least, were well rewarded — for they, too, were 'our people' and, all things being equal, they got the job. In theory, 'our people' included 'our separated brethren' in the North, Catholic and Protestant; in practice, the Protestants were only notionally 'ours' and some of the Catholics were doubtful, to say the least. In the last resort they, like everyone else, must undergo the litmus test of attitude to the party before being admitted to membership of the community — a test which Haughey was to apply to the Social Democratic and Labour Party in November 1985 following the signature of a new Anglo-Irish agreement which gave the Republic a formal role in Northern affairs.

The party, which set out to achieve the ideal of Davis, found itself limited by the very power it had worked so hard to attain. Or, perhaps, it became convinced that in order to keep that power, which was essential if it was to proceed step by step with the dismantling of the apparatus that bound the State to Britain, it must act more cautiously than it had ever believed would be the case. That meant, essentially, accepting the limitations of the State. De Valera had warned them that they must face the facts, meeting conditions as they existed and not as they would like them to be, so scaling down their ambitions to the point where aims were reduced to aspirations.

Whether or not they ever really meant to adopt Davis's view of a society in which Catholics, Protestants and people of other religions or of none might live together in harmony is debatable. Seán T. O'Kelly's claim, in 1929, that the party spoke 'for the big body of Catholic opinion . . . represented the big element of Catholicity' was ominous. So was de Valera's support for Mayo county council two years later when a librarian, who'd been appointed by a commission set up to eliminate jobbery and favouritism, was refused approval by the council because she was a Protestant. The government disbanded the council but was forced by a boycott of libraries in the county to tranfer the librarian to Dublin. In the Dáil, de Valera said: 'The people of Mayo, in a county where, I think . . . over 98 per cent of the population is Catholic, are justified in insisting on a Catholic librarian.' In the 'eighties this argument was used by Catholic fundamentalists, including some bishops, in support of their case for what amounted to Catholic legislation for a Catholic State and people. The party endorsed the argument and entered a new alignment with the bishops.

It had been argued that, during its early years in opposition, the party was attempting to make respectable those people who had been condemned with bell, book and candle by a bishops' pastoral less than a decade earlier: 'The guerilla war now being conducted by the Irregulars is without moral sanction and, therefore, the killing of National soldiers in the course of it is murder before God, the seizing of public and private property is robbery, the breaking of roads, bridges and railways is criminal destruction, the invasion of homes and the molestation of citizens a grevious crime.' It has also been claimed that, in making the old warriors respectable, the party was attempting to win the Catholic vote, or that part of the electorate which was influenced by the bishops. It certainly broadcast the suspicion that Cumann na nGaedheal was supported by Freemasons — a bid for the anti-Masonic vote? — and complained when the government forgot to inform the bishops that it was about to exchange diplomatic representatives with the Vatican. And no sooner was Fianna Fáil in power than two of its Ministers, P. J. Ruttledge and P. J. Little (then a Parliamentary Secretary), set off on a pilgrimage to Lourdes. De Valera declared Ireland a Catholic nation, as if that could be in doubt in the year of the Eucharistic Congress.

The party — secretive, disciplined, all-embracing and aspirational — was prepared to do more than make its representatives respectable and consolidate its electoral appeal. It was to erect new barriers around 'our people' who from now on would be protected, industrially by tariffs, culturally by censorship and morally by prohibitions on divorce, contraception and crossroads dancing. They were geographically islanded. They would be historically unique. This, as much as de Valera's vision of an Ireland of rural simplicity, was to confine the party within the borders of the twenty-six counties and confirm the nature of the despised Free State. In vain would Peadar O'Donnell chide de Valera with his lost republicanism and Seán O'Faolain complain that no Northerner could feel attracted to such a society; they and like-minded critics could safely be ignored as anticlerical, anti-national and enemies of 'our people'.

But there were, even between the beginning of the 'thirties

and the end of the 'fifties, some glimmers of hope. As for instance, when the party in government firmly refused to be caught up in the hysteria that accompanied the Spanish Civil War. The hierarchy supported Franco and called attention to anti-clerical atrocities said to have been committed by the Spanish government. De Valera refused to withdraw recognition from the republican administration and, in a Non-Intervention Act, forbade Irish citizens to enlist on either side. This and his refusal to be drawn into an anti-communist crusade at home, where the bishops believed that Saor Éire and the IRA were intent on red revolution, suggested that, perhaps, he was the man to stand up to the Church and for what Tod Andrews called the Jacobin tradition in Irish republicanism. Again, in 1957, when the marital problems of a Catholic and a Protestant at Fethard-on-Sea, Co. Wexford, led to a boycott of Protestants, he said: 'I repudiate any suggestion that this boycott is typical of the attitude or conduct of our people . . . I beg of all who have regard for the fair name, good repute and well-being of our nation to use their influence to bring this deplorable affair to a speedy end.' But was the boycott, which he described as unjust and cruel, typical of the attitude of 'our people'? And to what extent, though in a form that was not so extreme, did the party's legislation in the 'thirties and its behaviour in the 'fifties, reflect their attitude?

In its legislation and its Constitution, Fianna Fáil proved itself as eager to defend Catholic moral standards – and as anxious to avoid confrontation with the bishops – as its predecessors had been. W. T. Cosgrave's Free State Constitution was characterised as liberal-democratic; de Valera's 1937 Constitution was obviously marked by Catholic thought in matters of education, divorce and the special position of the Catholic Church. In his seminal account of Church-State relations in modern Ireland, J. H. Whyte summarised the differences and similarities between the governments of Cosgrave and de Valera: 'Mr Cosgrave refused to legalise

47

divorce; Mr de Valera made it unconstitutional. Mr Cosgrave's government regulated films and books. Mr de Valera's regulated dance halls. Mr Cosgrave's government forbade propaganda for the use of contraceptives; Mr de Valera's banned their sale or import. In all this they had the support of the third party in Irish politics, the Labour Party.'

In the 'fifties and 'sixties, some senior members of Fianna Fáil liked to make much of their resistance to clerical influence and the contrast between their independence and the loyalty demonstrated by Fine Gael. It was a curious kind of resistance and independence, usually expressed privately in the manner of Brendan Behan's daylight atheists. And in the 'eighties the roles were reversed as relations between Church and State, religion and politics, once more showed signs of becoming inextricably entangled.

It is sometimes said, on behalf of the leaders of the 'thirties, 'forties and 'fifties, that they had no option but to bend to the bishops' wishes and, on behalf of de Valera and the 'old team', that no other party would have managed to keep more than a hairsbreath between Church and State. But when the politicians chose to stand apart from the bishops, as they did during the Spanish Civil War, they succeeded in doing so without being penalised by the electorate or, indeed, by any less resistible force. In truth, they gave way to episcopal authority more often than they resisted it and almost invariably on social/moral issues where sexuality and the rights of minorities were involved. Historians are now beginning to argue that, between the 'twenties and the 'fifties, 'sexual immorality' became something of an ideological scapegoat; that the old political threat to our national integrity was replaced by a moral threat to our national Catholic purity. Fianna Fáil, which was given full credit by O'Faolain and others for its housing and welfare programmes, succumbed to this vision of a new enemy replacing the old coloniser, thus narrowing still further the definition of 'our people' and marking another step in its departure from the spirit of the nation. Many who considered themselves nationalists and genuinely favoured unity discovered that it was more comfortable to live within the confines of a Catholic state than to brave the open seas of unity and diversity. As time went on they became unwilling or afraid to make the concessions which reunification would involve. This unwillingness to make concessions — accompanied in some cases by a refusal to acknowledge that concessions might even be relevant — was to be underlined during the debate on a constitutional amendment on abortion in 1983 and in some of the public deliberations of the New Ireland Forum which attempted to construct a fresh nationalist approach to the issue of unity in the same year.

As for the claim that Fianna Fáil in its early years was more resistant to clerical influence than other parties: it could hardly have been less so, but then no other party made anything of either its ability or its willingness to resist. No other major party had presented itself as heir to the nation of Davis or the republic of Tone. And no other party was so long in office. In fact, its most blatant acceptance of Catholic nationalism and episcopal influence occurred not when it was in power but when it was in opposition and might have been expected to use the relative freedom which this permitted to strike a blow for the Republic. Instead, it took the opportunity to nudge a tottering government over the precipice and ignored the consequences for relations with the North or the Church.

To blame Fianna Fáil for the betrayal of Noel Browne by his party and cabinet colleagues in the Mother and Child Scheme debâcle of 1951 would be a travesty. But the party's astute aloofness, which was how John A. Murphy described de Valera's attitude to the affair, simply played into the hands of those who argued that the twenty-six county State was ruled from Rome, Maynooth or Archbishop's house in Dublin and that the politicians, with the honourable exception of Browne, were acquiescent to clerical control. 'The whole situation was mishandled,' Lemass was to tell Michael Mills of the *Irish Press* years later. 'I am not so sure that it was not allowed to develop in this way because the Coalition leaders were anxious to get an excuse to drop Noel Browne.' The argument was disingenuous. Browne was undoubtedly at loggerheads with the leadership of his own party, Clann na Poblachta. The Taoiseach, John A. Costello of Fine Gael, was certainly prepared to accept the hierarchy's opinion that the scheme transferred responsibility from the family to the State by making maternity and other health services freely available to everyone. In cabinet, only one Minister, Michael Keyes of Labour, is thought to have supported Browne and in public members of the government rushed to assure the bishops and the electorate, in the humblest terms, of their loyalty to the Church. In the Dáil de Valera uttered only one sentence on the affair: 'We have heard enough.'

What was at stake, then as in the 'eighties was the sovereign government's right to govern without interference, though in 1951 few commentators saw the conflict in such obvious terms. Some thought it a blunder, others an inevitable consequence of coalition. But the affair was to have deep and lasting effects, muddying attitudes to social justice, Church-State relations and unity, for years. Its immediate impact was on the government, which subsided in ignominy, and on Clann na Poblachta, which went into an irreversible decline. Later commentators wondered how a party such as Fianna Fáil, which proclaimed itself to be in the Wolfe Tone tradition, dedicated to uniting Protestant, Catholic and Dissenter in the common name of Irishman, could have remained aloof from a controversy which so clearly handed an opportunity to the opponents of unity. The answer is that, whatever about unity, it presented the party with an electoral advantage which it was determined to take. De Valera's astute aloofness maintained party unity and was electorally prudent. The damage to the prospects of national unity was of secondary importance.

50

One of the party's many astonishing characteristics, as we have seen, is its ability to ignore much contradictions. Impervious to criticism — while noting the names and numbers of the critics — it allows no element of self-doubt to invade its consciousness or to disturb the conviction that, as MacEntee said, it truly represented 'the idealism, the realism, the intelligence and the common sense of the great mass of all classes of the Irish people.' It is not as if, on all issues and on all occasions before the first leadership struggle, the party were united. Even the 'old team' had its rivalries and divisions. Gerry Boland returned the first £500 cheque which an outsider contributed to the party funds. Lemass retrieved it and happily accepted it for the party. Lemass and MacEntee conducted a vigorous debate on the Beveridge Report and whether or not something similar was appropriate to their State. (Lemass maintained it was.) Boland and Sean Moylan varied from sceptical to anti-clerical, MacEntee sought authorities on Catholic social thinking to support his arguments and Seán T. O'Kelly obeyed (but not for long) de Valera's instruction that Ministers should quit the Knights of St Columbanus. One member of the Cabinet (John Bowman suspects Jim Ryan) described another (Frank Aiken) as ignorant and obstinate, while Joseph Connolly, the first Minister for Lands, wrote that de Valera only wanted yes-men around him. Lemass and Paddy Smith, who was Minister for Agriculture, argued furiously about the relative merits of farming and industry and about the importance which Lemass attached to winning the support of the trade unions; Smith resigned. But despite such disagreements, Smith's resignation apart, little enough of this became common knowledge and some of the views held by their Ministers were not even suspected by the party faithful. Lemass, for some curious reason, insisted on arguing publicly about Beveridge from a point of view which was quite at odds with his personal convictions. De Valera's injunction about membership of the knights (it embraced all secret societies) followed

51

an occasion when he was less hospitably treated than O'Kelly had been by an Archbishop whose town both had visited; but the pique, like the occasion was private. Connolly disagreed with de Valera about one of the leader's pet ideas, the distribution of land among the landless; and Moylan came close to heresy on this question when he suggested that it was pointless giving land to people who had neither the means nor the ability to use it. Heresy, because the party still (in the late 'thirties) clung to the popular image of a largely rural organisation with, among its staunchest supporters, the very picture of 'our people', the small farmers and the men of no property. Connolly wrote of his differences with de Valera after his (Connolly's) departure from office but, by and large, the signs of a widening gap between the rhetoric of opposition and the reality of government remained hidden.

The primacy of the party and the perceived infallibility of its leadership demanded it. Whatever inconsistencies might have to be endured, the face of unity would be maintained. The leadership of de Valera, with its combination of authority, solemnity and paternalism, was central to the notion of 'our people': to the equation of people, party, faith and nation must be added, quite simply, the Chief. He may not have been the author of all of the party's policies, but he was the creator of its conscience and time and again felt compelled to insist that above all, he was no outsider. 'I have been brought up amongst the Irish people. I was reared in a labourer's cottage here in Ireland,' he said on the occasion of one of his best known and most characteristic statements. 'Whenever I wanted to know what the Irish people wanted I had only to examine my own heart and it told me straight off what the Irish people wanted.' Taken out of context, this could be made to sound egotistical. T. Ryle Dwyer totted up the number of times he used the personal pronoun 'I' in the course of that speech, which occupied four pages of the Dáil report; it came to 134. But it was a speech delivered in response to prodding by the *Freeman's Journal*, which had cast doubt on his credentials as an Irishman during the Treaty debates. It was the kind of nagging, irrelevant criticism which roused him to passion. Ten years later, to the charge that he was not really Irish, his enemies added the equally spurious claim that he was the bastard son of a Spanish Jew. 'There is not, so far as I know, a single drop of Jewish blood in my veins,' he replied. 'On both sides I come from Catholic stock. My father and mother were married in a Catholic church on 19 September 1881. I was born in October 1882. I was baptised in a Catholic church. I was brought up here in a Catholic home.' The equation of people, party, faith and nation was his, not suddenly produced as if it were the solution to some mathematical problem but reached, as if by osmosis, over years of meeting such charges, responding to everyday malice in everyday language. Of course, he was not without guile, any more than the people of East Limerick were.

Conor Cruise O'Brien, whose uncle, Father Eugene Sheehy, taught de Valera history, observed how, in office, he 'succeeded in the difficult feat of reassuring people who had been frightened of him without unduly disappointing his original followers'. His Church policy was, in Cruise O'Brien's view, a case in point. O'Faolain thought the clue to his success on the hustings was that he was always 'a combination of realism, sentimentality and ruthlessness, in which each was always corrupting the other'. He exhibited realism in his espousal of parliamentary democracy and ruthlessness, in the way he chose to deal with the IRA. Was the idea of 'our people' an example of his sentimentality and guile? Of preternatural cunning, the quality which Parnell was thought to possess? Or was it a flag of convenience, which could be flown at the party's discretion, over what its propagandist songwriters had so lately mocked as 'three-quarters of a nation'?

5

Localism

Nothing signalled the party's determination to stay in power more clearly than its willingness to trim, tack or change course when the need arose. It had an ability to do so as if it were the most natural thing in the world, as if every move were bringing closer the achievement of its ultimate ambition. There were always sound, pragmatic reasons for the change; delivered by de Valera in his convoluted, inelegant but homely style — could such tortuous reasoning be inspired by base motives? — or by Lemass, who always gave the impression that he knew what he was about, even when he was candidly admitting that he'd been wrong. In the long run, it would be for the best. So the party donned the cloak of Catholic nationalism with as little ceremony as it was to shed the aspiration to self-sufficiency, and for the few who hung back there were the thousands who accepted that this must be the way. The party succeeded, partly because of the weakness and incredibility of the opposition. Fine Gael could scarcely complain with conviction that in many ways Fianna Fáil was coming to resemble Fine Gael itself. Labour was divided, on the national question and on urban-rural lines. Fianna Fáil could point to the experience of the 'fifties as evidence that coalitions of Fine Gael and Labour did not work while relying on its own, broadly-based coalition to ensure that it had electoral support from all quarters. It embraced conservatives, reformers and even a few radicals; the most ardent Catholics with anti-clerical veterans and a scattering of Protestants and Jews. To the poor farmers and poorer farm labourers who were among its first supporters it was adding more and more men of property; and it managed to convince some trade union leaders and most union members that it represented their interests, if not exclusively, certainly more effectively than the Labour Party. Whatever the circumstances, it represented itself as more positive, more optimistic and closer to the *real* feelings of the people than anyone else.

It was a boast accompanied by rhetorical flourishes in which a mythical past and seven hundred years of oppression were interwoven with the promise of a glorious and united future. The fourth green field would be recovered, you could bet your life on that. But in the meantime Fianna Fáil was the party to look after the three green fields that we had: no-one could stand there and accuse them of not doing the right thing by the Irish people. And they did, after a fashion, do the right thing by the people they had promised to help, when what they needed was a labourer's cottage or a way out of the slums, a divide of land or a better pension. They took up where their predecessors had left the development of State enterprises — not necessarily because they believed in State enterprise but because native capitalists were not up to the task and the services were as essential to industry as the jobs were to the electorate. They provided grants for agriculture and protection for industry, though by the late 'thirties it was clear that agriculture could not hold, and industry could not absorb, the first generation to have reached maturity in an independent state. It was then that one of the most remarkable shifts in emphasis in the party's history occurred: Lemass, viewing this state of affairs with trepidation and fearing the consequences of mass emigration, convinced de Valera that he should, as Joseph Lee described it, preside over the subversion of the Ireland of his dreams. Instead of pursuing a vision of bucolic bliss, he should adopt a policy of rapid

55

industrialisation, which meant not only abandoning protection and notions of self-sufficiency but inviting foreign finance and industrial expertise to attempt a transformation which Irish capital had dismally failed to achieve. It was to take twenty years before the new policy emerged in the programmes for economic expansion, but in 1938 it had already been accepted by the advanced section of the party which Lemass represented that its survival — and the survival of the state — depended on radical change. De Valera, however reluctantly, agreed.

De Valera had never been totally opposed to industrialisation, provided its aim was self-sufficiency and the emphasis was on small communities. Between 1931 and 1938 industrial employment increased from 110,000 to 166,000; and unlike most industrialising countries, Ireland did not buy short-term growth at the price of a deterioration in working-class living standards. But de Valera was what the party resembled: a countryman who'd gone to work in the city but could never bring himself to think of it as home. He was suspicious of urban society and its influence which could be summed up in two words: modern and alien. It was the antithesis of his vision of the Golden Age and would certainly lead to demands which were at odds with his ideal of sturdy independence based on small farms. However, just as he had urged his followers to face facts in the 'twenties, he now had to admit that the flight from the land was a fact.

It is from the rural areas, and it is very difficult to see how people can be kept back on the farm. There is a big flow from villages, small towns and urban areas into the bigger centres. The smaller centres are diminishing. . . . That is a tendency for which I am sorry, but there is no use hoping that we can put back the clock. From the philosophical point of view, that might have been a better existence, because when all is said and done contentment is the thing that matters most.

56

Contentment and containment. De Valera still tried to keep expectations in check. In 1956, seventeen years after this acknowledgment of change, he was still arguing: 'The policy of self-reliance is the one policy that will enable our nation to continue to exist', and recalling how in 1917 he had told the people of Kilkenny: 'We have a choice. It may be that we have the choice of the humble cottage instead of the lackeys partaking of the sops in the big man's house.' His reluctance may have contributed to the delay of twenty years between recognition of the need for change and its formal adoption by the party. In the meantime, the Second World War was to offer de Valera a challenge to which he responded with resilience and statesmanship. Afterwards, there were to be two changes of government and the most debilitating haemorrhage of migration since the hungry 'seventies of the last century. Ironically, the war produced the economic isolation of which de Valera had once dreamed: if only the country were surrounded by a wall, he had said, he was satisfied it could 'maintain a population two or three times the size of our present population.'

In 1940, Ireland was cut off, but the population did not grow. More than ever, it was essential to keep the emigration routes open, lest the soaring numbers of unemployed threaten social stability. Here was a second and more telling irony, which was to be bitterly underscored in the decade that followed the isolation of the war. Even as de Valera talked about the choice of the humble cottage in preference to sops in the big man's house, tens of thousands of young men and women were abandoning their humble cottages for the bright lights of London, Birmingham and Coventry, Chicago, Boston and New York. Between 1951 and 1956, some 200,000 left; between 1956 and 1961, more than 212,000 followed, leaving the total population 5 per cent below what it had been when the State was founded.

Whether they went because they could not find work at home or because they could no longer stand the suffocating atmosphere of a state that seemed always to be shouting 'stop' was a question never asked. Whatever the cause, the consequences were the same. Desolate parishes, bleak and bedraggled villages, heartless little towns, all left to the old and the very young, and silence. Not the silence of contentment, but of ruin and dereliction.

How did the party — and, indeed, the State — survive this crisis? Largely, they survived not in spite of the emigrants' departure but because of it. As in other migrations, it was the most headstrong, vigorous and adventurous who led the way. As in other generations, the communities they left behind them were dispirited and leaderless. Very often, those who stayed were either weak or cagey or both. They played safe. What they had they held, and they practised as, in barely audible mutters, they preached: a shut mouth catches no flies. In the Four Glorious Years, there had been a big increase in the number of young people staying in Ireland because the emigration routes had been closed. (The intention was to encourage enlistment in the British Army.) The result, according to Tom Garvin, was: 'The two classic options open to a politicised young man in rural Ireland — voice, in the form of participation in militant politics, or exit, in the shape of emigration to America — had suddenly been reduced to one: voice.' In the 'fifties, it was the other classic option, emigration, that remained open; and the biggest irony of all was that it was to the advantage of Fianna Fáil that so many took it. There was a section of 'our people' which could, in time, be added to the sentimental list of exiles; for the moment, the party was relieved to see them go.

It would be naive to expect the relief to have been expressed in public statements or in speeches from election platforms. The only occasion on which the subject of emigration was raised by the party's spokesmen was when the blame could be laid at the door of the coalition governments. A minority within the party shared their leader's view that what ought to be of concern was the danger that the old

58

ways were being abandoned. Their views were summed up by a deputy from the Midlands, Michael Joe Kennedy, in a letter to Frank Gallagher, the author of a book about the Four Glorious Years, who had been the first editor of the *Irish Press* and was, in the 'fifties, head of the Government Information Bureau. 'The Land Commission had ceased to function except to collect annuities and two ministers are proclaiming in Hogan* style that there are too many people on the land . . . Our language policy is as dead as a dodo . . . We'll have English holiday camps in Gormanston etc., and beautiful international airports as sure as your name is Frank Gallagher. The Irish Ireland programme for schools will be watered down before Fianna Fáil quits office.' Kennedy's resentment may have been misdirected; his statement was prophetic. The party, however, was bent on other business.

Its survival in the 'fifties can only in part be attributed to the weakness of the opposition, the opportunism of its attitude to clerical interference and the safety-valve of emigration. Its roots were planted deep in the community, where its appeal to the past and its promise of a glorious future have always been matched by the unspectacular performance of the humdrum activities which the community has come to see as the duty of its politicians. Unspectacular and humdrum it may have been, the party's commitment to local affairs was pervasive – and effective, beyond the wildest fears of its amateurish and disorganised opponents. No task was too humble, or too personal, for its representatives, whether they were councillors, deputies or senators or, for that matter, the unelected custodians of the local organisation. The party may not have invented the phenomenon known to political scientists as localism, but its leading members in any county of the twenty-six must be sufficiently experienced practitioners to be able to give lessons in its operation.

---

*Paddy Hogan, a Cumann na nGaedheal Minister for Agriculture.

Localism takes many forms. Some of them are beneficial or harmless, other are not. In either case, they are the means by which a politician proves his commitment to his local community, 'our people' writ small, with the expectation that by doing so he will demonstrate his influence and increase his vote. De Valera did it, though it was hardly necessary, in Clare, by stringing placenames together in a familiar litany which, without another word, conjured memories of treasured wrongs and battles long ago. He was not in the business of doing favours for the constituency although, once in a while, he came, as his more reverent local followers put it, to hold confessions in Carmody's Hotel in Ennis. Once during the 'fifties, or so I was told by one of the leading Fianna Fáil businessmen in the town, a delegation of respectable citizens went to ask if he would use his influence to have a factory built in Clare. Their request was politely but peremptorily refused. It was not his job. 'The galling thing was,' said the businessman, 'no sooner was Lemass in power than the whole place was thriving.'

If de Valera retained the puritanism of old Sinn Féin, who regarded favours as the hallmark of Castle Catholics and their successors, de Valera's followers had no such inhibitions. All politicians, with the exception of an eccentric few, have come to accept the notion of service — or messenger-boy politics — on which the electorate insists over and above any other consideration. It is boring, time-consuming and largely unnecessary work, they readily admit, but woe betide anyone, from meekest backbencher to member of the cabinet, who fails to hold regular clinics or who refuses the roles of welfare officer, administrative go-between and wielder of influence in what the electorate sees as a complicated and usually crooked world. It was Fianna Fáil, particularly in its long years of uninterrupted rule, which turned localism of that kind into a craft and, with some help from the Fine Gael veteran, Oliver J. Flanagan, the concomitant business of letter-writing into a political art.

The favours sought of deputies varied from the crazy to the criminal. One of the party's long-serving members in Cork was discovered, in the 'seventies, to have promised an (albeit short) tarred road and a culvert to a constituent in dubious circumstances. During one of the debates on social/moral issues in the 'eighties, Noel Davern of Tipperary, later a member of the European Parliament, allowed a couple of journalists to examine a week's mail for first-hand evidence of the pressure then being placed on politicians to support a particular line. The evidence of concerted pressure was there, all right. So were the usual appeals for help with pensions, houses, grants and jobs — and there was a football pools coupon, half-filled which he was asked to complete by someone who 'always gives you the number one', with eternal loyalty promised if his forecast proved correct. The lively old Kerry deputy, 'Chub' O'Connor, made no secret of the fact that he kept a black book in which favours were noted, so that he wouldn't forget when he called on people during elections and they could be reminded too. One woman who wrote to two deputies about her case got the envelopes mixed up and sent each of them the letter intended for the other. The trouble was that she'd told both of them that she gave *him* her 'number one' and would never vote for anyone else, whatever happened. They sent her a joint reply, thanking her for the support and, no doubt, hoping that she'd continue her practice of double-voting in the future.

Multi-seat constituencies present special problems, with two or three of the party's deputies competing with each other even more fiercely than they compete with the opposition. A Fianna Fáil organiser once made the mistake of installing two men from the same Kerry constituency in one cramped Leinster House office. Rivalry begat piracy: all the lazier deputy had to do was to listen to his more energetic colleague dictating letters to constituents and make a note of the details. Half-an-hour later he'd fire off his own letter, knowing that the constituent would give him at least a share of the credit for taking up his case, unasked. The energetic deputy was enraged. It took him a couple of weeks to resolve the problem, but he is a resourceful man; and one Tuesday evening when the lazy fellow sat, with pencil poised as usual, he found that the essential bits of the letter were missing. On the way over from the railway station the clever one had bought a packet of postcards on which he'd written the names and addresses of his clients, and when he got to that part of the letter he'd take out the appropriate card, hold it up before the typist and then (to make assurance doubly sure) put it back in his pocket. He was still in the Dáil in the middle 'eighties.

Far from disapproving of Fianna Fáil's expert localism, the deputies of other parties began to envy its reputation for being able to get things done and, in due course, to emulate its performance. A Labour deputy in the 'eighties found the competition so stiff that, with each batch of letters he sent out, he would include one addressed to himself. That way, he could tell when his other letters arrived and knew that it was time to call on his lucky constituents 'to drive home my point'. When they are not writing letters or holding clinics, many politicians are busy attending local functions of all sorts, paying special attention to funerals. One of the much-admired authorities in this area was Paddy Burke of north Dublin whose son, Ray, was to become an astute and effective Minister. Burke the elder, who was known as the bishop, never missed a local funeral. There was, however, one occasion when a Fine Gael man arrived at a church and noted that Burke wasn't already in action, gliding from mourner to mourner, shaking hands. The ceremony came to an end and still the bishop was nowhere to be seen. The Fine Gael man was beginning to feel triumphant as the priest led the procession down the aisle; but suddenly there was the bishop in his wake, swinging a thurible among the altar boys! 'You can't beat experience,' Fianna Fáil men would say, re-telling the story with obvious delight.

Not all of their exploits were so innocent or so amusing. 'Fianna Fáil is a great organisation; so is the Mafia,' was the opening sentence of a leading article in *The Irish Times* during the 'sixties. There were tales of planning permission that had been 'swung', jobs that had been arranged and land or property deals that had been pulled off with the help of inside information. Occasionally there was a fuss, as when Haughey sold his home and a 40-acre farm in 1969 for £204,000, after planning permission had been obtained for the land, or when Seán Doherty, who was Minister for Justice in 1982, was accused of undue interference in garda affairs. Meanwhile the legend of 'strokes' and the cult of 'the cute hoor' helped to enhance the reputations of some of the party's best-known members as 'operators'. In many cases it was hard to tell whether stories were put about by a man's enemies in order to ruin him or by his friends to save him from ruin. Donagh O'Malley liked to spread stories of a somewhat different character about himself. One was about being stopped as he drove up a one-way street. 'Did yeh not see the arrows?' the guard asked him. 'To tell you the truth, sergeant,' said O'Malley, 'I didn't even see the fucking Indians.' As he might have said, it probably helped to take the harm out of a more menacing remark which was also attributed to him. This, too, was addressed to a guard, in a pub after hours: 'Do you want a pint or a transfer?'

'Parties like Fianna Fáil tend to have debts to pay, if only in the form of rewards for the loyal services of large numbers of activists,' Tom Garvin writes, noting that Tammany Hall-style practices are held to be particularly likely when one party has a monopoly or near-monopoly of executive power. But he also notes that two studies in local affairs — one in Neil Blaney's Donegal constituency, the other in Munster — produced contradictory results. He comments: 'There is, for what it is worth, a rich folklore concerning petty patronage and also, at a slightly more serious level, concerning irregular allocations of public housing and planning permissions. It is difficult, however, to be able to distinguish clearly between patronage and *bona fide* meritocratic practice in many cases.' That may be so, though to the unscientific observer it looks suspiciously as if at least some politicians have managed to construct fiefdoms for themselves, trading favours for votes in much the same way as, in the last century, the classic gombeen merchant traded loans for land.

Fiefdoms and dynasties. There is no doubt at all that, at least in a substantial minority of cases, seats are kept in the family. As people are born into the party – in the sense that they inherit their parents' political allegiance – so they are likely to pass on their local power and influence to one or more of their relatives. This is also true of Fine Gael, but to a lesser extent; it is an even more pronounced tendency among members of the Labour Party. But Fianna Fáil from the start – unlike either Cumann na nGaedheal or Sinn Féin – made a virtue of choosing candidates who lived in their constituencies and came from families that were active in local affairs. David M. Farrell, a researcher at the European University Institute of Florence, has been studying routes to the Dáil and the influence of localism. He reports a preference for 'sports heroes, relatives and political activists', especially in Fianna Fáil. Just over a quarter of all deputies who won seats in the three-in-a-row elections of the 1980s had had the advantage of political relations and among Fianna Fáil members the tally was 29 per cent: thirty of its 103 TDs in that period were the sons, daughters, nieces, nephews, widows, brothers or sons-in-law of deputies or senators. Almost one in five had been prominent in sport (many more, I believe, were involved in the administration of the GAA) and about two-thirds had experience in local government.

The party's success in localism reflected the strength of an organisation which, even before it came to power, had penetrated every parish in the State. In spite of the internal struggles of the 'eighties it still had more than 2,700 cumainn, or branches, on its books in 1984. The practice of localism not only reflected strength, it ensured that organisational muscles were toned-up between elections; 'keeping the boys on their toes' was how one of the national organisers saw it. The local organisation acted as the eyes and ears of the party, recording the reactions of the members and of voters generally to the party's performance. For decades, this was the process which enabled Fianna Fáil to claim with some justification that it *knew* what the people were thinking. The local organisation also acted, in a sense, as the party's mouthpiece, ensuring that messages from the top, which occasionally needed to be decoded, were transmitted with just the right emphasis (or dollop of obfuscation) to the members. If was a function that became much more complicated as leadership lost its invincible air and conflicting messages from the top turned local activists into foot-soldiers in an apparently endless internal campaign.

6

Lemass

The legend of Seán Lemass is that he emerged suddenly from de Valera's lengthening shadow to take the party and the State by the scruff of the neck and whisk both into the middle of the twentieth century. It's a tale, as told by some of his admirers, with an echo of the heroic, as if Fionn Mac Cumhail had reappeared, scooped up the land that was Lough Neagh and hurled it again into the Irish Sea to make a new island. De Valera, at least, would have been wryly amused.

But the birth of modern Ireland was bound to be difficult. Twenty years separated de Valera's reluctant admission of failure at the end of the 'thirties and Lemass's arrival in office as Taoiseach and leader of the party; years in which we continued to hang a green curtain between ourselves and the world outside, hoping to prevent our protected people from catching sight of the foreign bogeyman and to prevent him from gaining a toehold on our soil, only to discover that half-a-million of those whom we had wished to protect had gone to live with the foreigner and the only option that remained open to those at home was to invite him in. They were years of attrition during which the argument for change was hammered in with the monotony of trains rumbling to the mail-boat and hammered home when they rumbled back with holiday stories of tempting delights.

'Ah Brendan, it must be marvellous to feel free,' a customs officer greeted the young Behan on his way home from Borstal. 'Aye, it must,' said Behan, passing on into what he called our paper republic. There were hundreds of thousands who, had they heard him, would have shrugged in agreement.

The argument for change was undeniable and Lemass used it, not merely to detach himself from the past but to prepare the State for the future. It was his good fortune that he inherited some innovative schemes and institutions from Coalition predecessors and enjoyed a creatively argumentative relationship with Ken Whitaker, a deeply thoughtful civil servant whom his predecessors had appointed to a key position in the Department of Finance. He also inherited a party which was still in the hands of the 'old team' and bore the marks of their rigidity; he was the last of their generation and the first of the new men to whom they finally, grudgingly relinquished control. When Lemass became Taoiseach, most of de Valera's original Ministers still held office and in the Dáil, a quarter of the deputies were over sixty years of age, 60 per cent of them over forty-five. The party, which he had helped to establish when he was 27, had run out of steam and he could scarcely be blamed if, twenty to thirty years on, he showed signs of running out of patience. He was convinced that de Valera had mistimed the 1948 election, taking fright at the emergence of Clann na Poblachta as a mirror image of Fianna Fáil. He was uneasy with the 'play safe' platform which the party adopted and more uncomfortable than most when it failed and he found himself in opposition. In government (1951-'54) he disagreed with Seán MacEntee's professed monetarism and was not surprised when the notoriously harsh budget of 1952 was followed by another defeat. He was to tell Michael Mills of the *Irish Press* that the party did not really begin to take stock of its position until that second period in opposition, by which he almost certainly meant that it was not until then that he came to grips with the conservative axis formed by MacEntee and Frank Aiken and began to wear down de Valera's resistance to change. At least, the second defeat helped to convince de Valera that the party could not survive without a strong urban base.

Fianna Fáil had also fought two elections on the issue of financial orthodoxy – and lost both. A crumb of comfort for Lemass who, whatever his sideways slides and inconsistencies, or his views about repatriating assets or balancing books, could never be accused of orthodoxy.

Lemass was at his most irritable – and most inconsistent – when he was thrust into opposition and had to watch others attempting what he wanted to achieve, especially in his beloved Department of Industry and Commerce. 'When we get back we'll get rid of this piece of rubbish,' he snapped after Dan Morrissey of the first Inter-Party government had announced the establishment of the Industrial Development Authority. The efforts of Bill Norton of Labour were equally summarily dismissed in the 'fifties. He set out to encourage foreign capital and argued that war-time tariffs had merely helped 'these boys' (meaning protected industry) to make money. He was denounced as anti-national, as loudly by Lemass as by de Valera who complained of foreigners being 'festooned with tax reliefs' and preached the need to keep Ireland for the Irish. De Valera's criticism was predictable, but Lemass had been – and was again – the apostle of free trade and foreign investment, which the IDA actively promoted. It is the role on which his reputation rests. Lemass made light of such contradictions. He justified his opposition to the IDA on the grounds that Morrissey's proposals were discriminatory; anyway, he did not want 'a gang of crackpot socialist planners' on the board. As for foreign investment, the timing was wrong, though Lemass himself had called for a programme of development employing private, public *and foreign* capital three years earlier. Other explanations are offered by commentators who suggest, for example, that Lemass had difficulty coming to terms with such departures from traditional policy; it is much more likely that he was intent on preserving party unity and on using whatever opportunity presented itself to take on the opposition, in this case a shaky Coalition governing a country that was clearly in crisis. He was sure that Fianna Fáil could do better; to see that it got the chance, it was his duty to oppose. It was, some would say, Lemass's style.

De Valera had a convoluted style of speaking and was often accused of saying more or less (or something other) than he intended to say. It was what people expected of an intellectual and daemonic leader. The fact that he thought and talked like a countryman, no more fluently and no more clearly, was forgotten. Lemass was, as the Americans say, street-wise. A cityman through and through, he knew his way around before the Civil War and the party made a politician of him. His style of speaking was matter-of-fact, business-like and to the point. People admired his direct-ness and took him at face value. He was a man of action and that, too, was admired by young people, sometimes uncritically and always in contrast to his complicated pre-decessor. De Valera was once asked if he'd read Machiavelli. He hadn't, but he knew what Machiavelli had written and found it interesting. No one, as far as we know, ever asked Lemass about Machiavelli's Prince, but he played the part at least as often and arguably with more success than Dev. As he wound his tortuous way from stubborn defence of pro-tectionism to the apostasy of free trade, he made canny use of nationalist rhetoric not only to confound opposition but to undermine some of the basic tenets of nationalism. How he made his case at a given time depended on where the opposition was coming from, on whether the party was in power or not and on whether, at that stage of his campaign, he was advancing or retreating. To use a sporting metaphor, he never took his eye off the ball. De Valera had his dreams and was enough of a realist to admit that in the end they were beyond his reach. Lemass had his targets and was enough of a dreamer to set a five-year deadline for their achievement. He nearly made it.

He was also, as indicated above, a considerable tactician who was capable of giving a nod in the direction of de

Valera's dreams when circumstances or the party demanded. 'Independence,' he once told the people of Tipperary, 'will still need to call upon the capacity for high endeavour and unrestrained patriotism that we find in Tipperary — perhaps even for another contribution from their undoubted store of valour.' In the territory of Dan Breen and Seán Forde, it sounded remarkably like incitement, but that was in the 'fifties and the party, in opposition, had taken its customary swerve into the greenery. Lemass's modernisation was not the stuff of an anti-partition rally. By 1957, target and dream had been fused and it was possible, because the Coalition could be held responsible, to mention emigration: 'We must not allow that faith of ours [in unity] to be weakened by the present unnecessary depression, but we have to prove it to be justified by practical results in the twenty-six counties — 95,000 unemployed and 60,000 emigrants per year are not good arguments for the ending of partition.' It was a case of the dream justifying the target.

Lemass's statement that 'a rising tide lifts all boats' has been interpreted by many critics as an indication that he was careless of social matters and by some of his less scrupulous supporters as a justification for downright callousness in the guise of rough-and-tumble enterprise. Here, again, we find a Machiavellian touch. Lemass had little sympathy for the hard-faced capitalist approach to either social policies in general or labour relations in particular. His various Conditions of Employment Acts produced considerable improvements in working conditions. In a long-running debate in cabinet, however, Lemass went much further than many commentators imagined, arguing doggedly for progress along the lines of the Beveridge Report which, among other things, prepared the ground for the British welfare state system. It was a fascinating debate: de Valera and MacEntee, on one side, diligently leafed through learned magazines for theological arguments from Catholic social theory to oppose the report. They came up with an authority who turned out to be an enthusiastic supporter of the Portuguese dictator, Salazar. Lemass, on the other side, quoted John Maynard Keynes and Nicholas Kalder, advisers to the British government, in support of an improved welfare system, more state intervention in the economy and a greater role for the trade unions. While senior civil servants supplied Ministers with memoranda reminding them that Labour in the Republic was likely to gain as a result of Britain's adoption of many of Beveridge's recommendations, Lemass was insisting that, once the new system had been introduced in the North, the difference between the two parts of the country would become even more pronounced. However, for reasons which have not been explained, Lemass's public contributions to this debate harped on what the country could afford. A conciliatory gesture to his cabinet opponents? An attempt to preserve at least the appearance of party unity? Or Lemass's version of de Valera's frugal comfort consciously deflating expectations?

The reasons behind the public statements were obscure; they may have been tactical. The results, however, were clear. Lemass was attacked by the Labour Party and suspected by the unions of having abandoned a hitherto sympathetic attitude to them. Their anger was gradually assuaged, partly because their reaction to his developing and occasionally contradictory ideas was neither coherent nor uniform and partly because he seemed willing to take on other elements of Irish society — the banks, industry and farmers — as well. He blamed the banks for lack of investment, industry for failing to take advantage of protection to become more efficient and productive, and the farmers for insisting that they should be helped at the expense of everyone else. He was accused by one industrialist, if not of being a communist then of flirting with communist ideas, because of his approach to state intervention, and by others of sectoral favouritism in his proposals for foreign investment and free trade.

Throughout the 'fifties he was also conducting a separate

but related debate with Whitaker who took a much more cautious line than he did, stressing the role of private enterprise rather than state intervention and advocating methods of increasing production rather than direct and immediate action to provide employment. Whitaker's report on economic development, which was submitted to the government in 1958, charted a course of financial orthodoxy, opposed financial expedients and the setting of fanciful targets and was described by one commentator as 'no more than the intelligent application to the local Irish situation of doctrines that had been current among economists elsewhere for many years'. Lemass took note of Whitaker's cautionary tone and, to take one example, agreed to submerge 'the question of employment in the wider question of the need for a redefinition of economic policy brought about by the prospect of free trade'.

David Thornley, historian, political commentator and later a Labour deputy, set Lemass's debates in this context: 'A devoted handful of twentieth-century men essay the painful, uphill struggle of educating their followers to the realisation that growth rates and schools are more important than getting a boreen macadammed or fixing a road mender's job.' Obviously there was not much joy in it for the masters of localism. People were, in Thornley's view, uneducated, apathetic, grasping for a little prosperity: 'Our people have a vague comprehension that we must be competitive now, just as we had to be protected in the 'thirties and 'forties. But are they being educated to the full implications of this revolution?

The answer to this question, which Thornley posed in 1964, is that the people were not being educated to the full implications of Lemass's revolution. Some would say that Lemass was too preoccupied with the business of educating their industrial and political leaders, whose mediocrity and caution were matched only by their determination to get what they could from Lemass's changes without having to pay the price of increased efficiency or more adventurous

72

policies. The same leaders were to demonstrate the same qualities of stubborness and greed when Ireland eventually joined the EEC and their short-sighted attitudes cost many Irish workers their jobs. Lemass, it was thought in the early 'sixties, was to face a long, hard slog before — if ever — he had his way. But instead of a grinding siege there was a series of running battles and a lot of sniping as he picked off some critics and outmanoeuvred others. He gradually involved the unions in committees set up to examine the state of industry and advise on preparations for free trade. (A union official was to complain in the Dáil that, with the burden of committee work which Lemass had given them, his colleagues had little time for anything else.) He ran into trouble with a pay pause for the public service in 1963 but escaped by intervening in the wage negotiations of the following year, actually securing a settlement that was larger than the employers were prepared to offer. He shrewdly separated the questions of free trade and foreign investment, so ensuring that his critics on the industrial front were divided; he argued that free trade was inevitable and foreign investment, especially if employed in joint ventures, would be a help, not a hindrance to Irish companies. He continued to chivvy the banks for investment but probably gave up his hope that the years of protection and isolation had produced a pool of managerial talent capable of taking advantage of more competitive conditions. 'The managerial pool was choked with weeds,' said one of his supporters. 'The whines from motley interests exposed to the threat of competition do not suggest an elite entrepreneurial cadre anxious to conquer new worlds.'

Lemass, in all of his arguments, used to the full the urgency created by the imminence of free trade and by the social and economic crisis of the 'fifties. He persuaded his audience that, sooner or later, Ireland must join one of the major European trading areas: her application for membership of the European Economic Community was made in 1961 but lapsed when de Gaulle vetoed Britain's application in 1963 and was not to be revived until after Lemass had retired. In 1965 he led the successful negotiation of an Anglo-Irish Free Trade Area, which was due to be fully effective by 1976. Fine Gael, by and large, accepted his arguments; the Labour Party did not.

Inside Fianna Fáil, Lemass was regarded with some suspicion in the early years of his campaign. The debate with MacEntee, however, was conducted almost exclusively in the privacy of the cabinet and in memoranda circulated by competing departments, Finance and Industry and Commerce. Erskine Childers made a couple of brief public appearances on MacEntee's platform; Lemass had the support of Seán Moylan, one of the first Ministers to question the wisdom of the party's agrarian policies. Only once did resistance to Lemass lead to an open break, when Paddy Smith of Cavan resigned as Minister for Agriculture in 1964 because he believed the Taoiseach was paying too much attention to the unions and too little to the farmers. Smith told me many years later how he came to see the wage negotiations of early 1964 as the last straw and, much though he respected Lemass, decided to quit. Lemass's reaction was characteristic: 'I was no sooner out of the office,' said Smith, with only slight exaggeration, 'than he had Charlie Haughey appointed in my place.'

Kevin Boland, in *Up Dev* and *The Rise and Decline of Fianna Fáil*, reflects the frustrations of those who not only viewed Lemass's modernisation with suspicion but disliked his reliance on foreign capitalists as well. In *Up Dev* he writes:

Mr Lemass did make an effort to get the investment postulated in his 'Hundred Thousand Jobs' document from the entrepreneurial class developed by his protectionist policy, but he found that patriotism was in short supply in that sector, where the highest patriotic aspiration was to win or breed the winner of the Derby or the Cheltenham Gold Cup — for the glory of old Ireland. In

74

the disastrous state of the economy at the time, he couldn't wait and the attraction of external investment became the national aim. I was bewildered and shocked to find that the principle of Irish ownership of industry, which was central to the Republican policy as I had always understood it, was gone, but I must admit I was ill-equipped to argue with those who had borne the heat of the day and I had thousands of ill-housed and under-nourished people in my constituency to whom I could not say 'live horse and you'll get grass'.

When the First Programme for Economic Expansion was announced by Lemass at the party's ard-fheis in 1958 the delegates were enthusiastic and the *Irish Press* ecstatic. Its headline exaggerated the amount of expenditure involved by a couple of hundred per cent. Some Fianna Fáil spokes-men, however, were slow to take credit for the programme which, they insisted, was the work of civil servants, there-fore non-political or, at any rate, non-partisan. Lemass would have no truck with such caution. 'The one thing civil servants won't do', he said later, 'is take decisions. They are not trained to do this. This is the difference between the bureaucrat and the politician.' It was also the difference between Lemass and some of his colleagues.

The programme was hailed as a landmark in Irish econ-omic history. For the first time the government had set out a comprehensive statement of its policies and objectives, not just for one year ahead but for the following five years. Frankly admitting that self-sufficiency had failed, the pro-gramme called for a change in policy, stressed the need for agriculture and industry to modernise, so that they could compete in world markets and looked forward to the arrival of free trade as an opportunity for Ireland to participate in worldwide growth.

The shift from protection to competition usually proves politically traumatic and, in this case, posed both ideological

75

and practical problems for the party. Had circumstances been different, these problems might have blocked the reversal of hallowed policies, but the circumstances were desperate and Lemass exploited them with the skill and courage of a true adventurer. There were, of course, many criticisms of the first and second programmes: they were not programmes, let alone plans, according to Declan Costello of Fine Gael, and academic critics have pointed out that, as forecasts of the economy's development, they were 'extremely poor' – and 'not even very accurate as a summary of the government's own policies'. But the First Programme in particular was indeed a landmark and its introduction was relatively trouble-free.

The First Programme was not debated in the Dáil, but when the closely related business of the Anglo-Irish free trade area was discussed in 1966, the fiftieth anniversary of the Rising, it was a Labour deputy, Seán Treacy, who took refuge in nationalist rhetoric. What had been done, he said, was 'more final, more binding and irrevocable than the Charter of Henry II or the Act of Union.' Whether it was a victory of experts over bureaucrats, the triumph of one set of bourgeois politicians over another or a new Act of Union, Lemass's achievement had a profound impact on Irish life; it was a high point in the history of the party and the State. Without it, both would have been put at risk in the 'sixties and the poorer, less optimistic decades since.

7

The Men in the Mohair Suits

Seán Lemass, it was said, moved like a young man in a hurry. But he was not a young man: almost sixty when he became leader of the party in 1959, his hurry was not the impetuous haste of youth but the urgency of someone who saw that time was running out, for the party and the State. He had come to power, not after a quick contest but at the end of a long struggle conducted with assiduous political skill against the most tenacious members of the 'old team'. We have seen how he overcame the opposition of de Valera, MacEntee and Aiken on economic policy. We will look again at how he changed attitudes on the national question. These were the great public issues of an extraordinary career.

Lemass, however, fought and won another fierce internal struggle to put his stamp on the party. Here, his opponent was an old comrade from the years in which, with de Valera and Tommy Mullins, they tramped the country setting up the organisation. Gerry Boland who saw himself as, in many ways, the keeper of the party's conscience, resented and resisted Lemass's every attempt at change. The first big cheque the party received from an outsider provoked a rift between them. The cheque for £500 came from Joe McGrath of the Irish Hospitals Sweepstakes, a friend of Lemass but one who had taken the pro-Treaty side in the Civil War. Boland promptly sent it back. Lemass had the cheque redirected to him: when it came to fighting elections, *all* contributions were welcome. Kevin Boland recalls: 'My father could see the gradual change in character [of the party] from then on and watched futilely while it developed.' In fact, his father's disagreements with Lemass went far beyond fundraising and who was or was not an acceptable contributor. Boland believed in industrial development based only on native raw materials and the skills of Irishmen. He was sceptical about the prospects of some industries that had been afforded protection but was even more suspicious of foreign investment and, as Kevin Boland put it, involvement with the entrepreneurial class.

Lemass saw Boland as a myopic old Sinn Féiner who failed to distinguish between the rhetoric of opposition and the reality of government. Lemass refused to concentrate on the Civil War as a source of political division, hardly ever used the Irish language and believed that to go on talking about partition, when no one intended to do anything about it, was a waste of energy. To him the argument was not about achieving independence but about the use that was to be made of the independence that had been achieved. In the end, he engineered the decision to drop Boland from the cabinet, thus increasing the bitterness between them, though de Valera appears to have made a deal with his departing comrade to prevent a prolonged and open row: Kevin Boland became a member of the cabinet on his first day in the Dáil in 1957.

Once he was firmly in control, Lemass eased out of office most other members of the 'old team' who did not go willingly. Eight of the thirteen members of de Valera's last cabinet had fought in the Civil War; in Lemass's last cabinet, seven years later, there were only three old warriors. It's significant, though, that two of the three survivors were MacEntee and Aiken, his sparring partners on social and economic affairs. Lemass could be impatiently critical of his colleagues – 'Will you look at what I have to work with,' he said to a younger man, when persuading him to take a post that might have gone to one of the elders – but he resisted the temptation to make a clean sweep. Clearly, in spite of his apparent haste, he recognised the value of continuity and of maintaining a balance between the different forces within the party; he respected, if he did not share, the vision of MacEntee and Aiken.

The impression of haste derived not merely from the changes that he wrought, some of which had begun before he became leader, but from the inevitable transfer of power to a new generation, a shift of emphasis to new issues and accompanying challenges to old values on several fronts. His revolution was essentially industrial, but the conversion of a society that had been deeply ingrained with rural values into one that took on a largely urban character could not have been achieved without a considerable psychological shock. Twenty years later, some of the tremors were still being felt, for the revolution asked as many questions as it answered and there was scarcely a corner of Irish life that it did not touch.

The boom of the 'sixties meant not just more and different jobs but a dramatic increase in consumer spending and demand, more imported goods, more foreigners in Ireland, whether as investors or tourists, more Irish people going abroad on holidays and eventually, for the first time ever, a wave of migrants coming home. Many of the foreign industries employed women, mainly or exclusively, and in places where few people had ever been able to find work women now achieved an albeit limited independence. Mobility gave young and old access to events far beyond their parish or county boundaries; travel was soon to lose the wonder that made an old Kerryman exclaim, as he was driven through Newbridge on the way to Dublin: 'Isn't it a terror to think there are so many people living so far away from home.' Seán O'Casey's view that all good things emerge from a regular wage packet seemed to be borne out.

Gradually, with the assistance of television (native and foreign, paid for or pirated) and a departure from traditionally unquestioning journalism, the cramped society of the 'fifties gave way to a more open life — at least, for those who could afford it. Issues of national and local importance were taken up by political commentators on 'Hurlers on the Ditch' and '7 Days' and by almost everyone on 'The Late Late Show'. In *The Irish Times*, John Healy's 'Backbencher' column shed an insider's light on the activities of politicians of both local and national importance; and women writing for all of the daily newspapers created an excitement which had been absent from journalism since the heyday of the *Irish Press*.

The incomparable Seán Ó Riada discovered an old link between Irish and European music and breathed new life into old airs. His admirers were to see his achievement as the first exploration of a new identity, the first sign of a cultural renaissance. It certainly added to the surge of confidence in what was once derided as 'servants' music' — a surge that had begun with the fleadhanna ceoil of the 'fifties and reached the cities by way of late-night concerts, singing pubs and groups like The Dubliners who gave the music an urban tone. In 'Ballrooms of Romance', the little bands that had played such plaintive airs as 'Moonlight in Mayo' and 'South of the Border' gave way to showbands, much as the halls themselves, which had grown from de Valera's ban on crossroads dancing, lost out to the bigger and jazzier Arcadias, Astorias and Olympics, many of them owned by a new generation of Fianna Fáil men.

Changes came more slowly to other shores. You could still, on a stroll around central Dublin, find yourself in the company of Patrick Kavanagh, Myles na Gopaleen or Brendan Behan, the walking wounded from the battles of the 'forties and 'fifties. Novels by John McGahern and Edna O'Brien, which emerged from that cramped society, were banned as indecent and obscene though there were few among their many Irish readers who had not shared their experience or would deny the accuracy of their observation. Television produced its moments of excruciating farce, as when a bishop phoned in to complain about a reference to a honeymooner's nightie and a young playwright called Brian Trevaskis found himself at the centre of scandal and controversy because he criticised Galway cathedral and the bishop who built it. More farcical still, when there were complaints about a programme on moneylenders, the government set up an inquiry — not into moneylending but into how the programme was made.

By and large, church-state relations were more relaxed in the 'sixties than they had been for a long time. John Whyte described the first half of the decade as a period of unwonted harmony. Lemass told Michael Mills that he had little occasion to meet the bishops, and the cardinal archbishop of Armagh, William Conway, said during an RTE interview that in his day-to-day dealings with politicians he had as much to do with Stormont as with the Republic. In any event, we must assume, the bishops were otherwise engaged: the second Vatican Council (1962-'65) and the reign of John XXIII, which ended in 1963, provoked uncertainty about the nature and durability of their own authority. It seemed as if the Pope, too, was intent on modernisation, introducing a system of shared responsibility where bleak authoritarianism had ruled. John Charles McQuaid, on his way home from the council, sought to reassure the Catholics of Ireland that nothing had changed; but change was in the air and, in Ireland, Lemass the moderniser was to find it to his advantage. The visit of John F. Kennedy, president of the United States, also increased the momentum. Among the staid old men who still filled most of the seats in Leinster House in 1963, he cut a boyish figure. If young people could run the most powerful country in the western world, what was to prevent them from running Ireland? And if Irish people could be so spectacularly successful when they went away, why not at home?

The new prosperity made room for a social conscience, a small but persistent voice during the second half of the 'sixties. It came stuttering into life with protests on the

81

streets about housing conditions and about the destruction of Dublin's Georgian buildings — demolished to provide space for ugly office blocks, built by speculators, occasionally with the government's assistance, and, in many cases, leased back to Departments of State to accommodate increasing numbers of public servants. Celebration of the fiftieth anniversary of the Rising provoked a debate, which began in quiet academic corners, about what independence meant and what it had achieved. As the supporters of tradition saw it, a revisionist school of history was born. The questions were asked, in a different form, by RTE's television programmes on the Rising. For the first time, James Connolly's influence began to be appreciated by more than a handful of historians and activists in movements of the left. The new consciousness of Connolly's socialism helped recruitment to the Labour Party; the questions raised about independence reinforced the case made by Lemass.

Changing the emphasis in the party from age and tradition to youth and adventure, he promoted two Ministers whom de Valera had appointed, Jack Lynch and Neil Blaney, retained Kevin Boland and introduced to his cabinet the men who were to be most closely identified with the period of economic boom: Charlie Haughey, George Colley, Brian Lenihan, Paddy Hillery and Donogh O'Malley. They enjoyed the prosperity that surrounded them, and some took their share of it in conspicuous style. Haughey, O'Malley and Lenihan held court in the Russell Hotel, usually in the company of builders, speculators and architects, self-made men, whose pleasure at having recently arrived in the easy elegance of another age was matched by their eagerness to take full advantage of their own — and, of course, to hear the latest from Leinster House down the road where O'Malley's gleeful assaults on the fuddy-duddy world of cautious civil servants and crusty old colleagues were the stuff of rumour and his own tall tales. The same tales might be re-told, with rich embroidery, by O'Malley himself when he dropped into the

Brazen Head or Cruise's Hotel in Limerick at weekends or by Lenihan on his regular visits to Groome's in Parnell Square, a hotel run, it sometimes seemed, for the benefit of an egalitarian company of Dublin's actors, politicians and stray writers by the unfailingly generous Patti Groome whose husband, Joe, was a founder member and vice-president of the party. They were an intriguing trio: Haughey, with his mocking, sardonic humour; O'Malley, who could never conceal his joy in life, and Lenihan, managing the marvellous feat of sounding bombastic and self-deprecating at once. They and their companions had a style that commanded attention, though not always the admiration of the people whose style they imitated. Most of the time they were too busy enjoying themselves to bother. Tim Pat Coogan coined a title for them: the men in the mohair suits.

Theirs was the face of Fianna Fáil which was most visible to the public. There were others, for what Lemass had done was not to build a new party but to add a storey to the old, much as the sons of the country men who had once waited for news of the Republic were now renovating their houses — removing the thatch to make way for a second storey and a new slate roof. A sign, people would have said a generation earlier, of money from America. Now, the money might well have come from America but it was earned in the factory down the road and the houses that it built were, in their ungainly way, symbols of the new order that was being superimposed on the old.

In the party, the rugged face of tradition was presented by Boland and Blaney, the hard men who looked after the organisation and stonewalled their critics in the Dáil. Blaney, the quintessential localist, with an inherited Donegal fiefdom in his pocket, was given credit for pulling the chestnuts out of many a by-election fire. But he departed from tradition, or Boland's version of it, in two ways. The first was in his role as spokesman for Taca, an elitist fundraising organisation of 500 businessmen who paid £100 a year and enjoyed ostentatious dinners in the Gresham Hotel. When they were not planning profitable coups, the mohair-suited men liked to turn up with the Tacateers to show the green flag, with the half-joke that they were doing it all for the ould party or the ould country. The second parting with tradition, for Blaney, was in the style of his victory celebrations. Long before anyone else in Irish politics dreamed of such lavish displays, he was leading motorcades in triumph across the Donegal countryside to his colleague, Bernard McGlinchey's Golden Grill saloon in Letterkenny. Bright ties, dark glasses and open cars, swaying with gum-chewing aides, were vivid reminders of another time, another place: the America of the old populist, Huey Long, governor of Louisiana.

Boland — ironically, he was one of Taca's officers — called the mohair-suited ones 'mohawks', and was suspicious of their airs. He nurtured a brand of patriotism that he'd learned from his formidable father. It was based on the dictum 'my party right or wrong' and the conviction that his side of the party was firmly in possession of the holy grail of republicanism. If some of his colleagues had little time for outsiders, Boland had none at all. 'The only way to deprive the wrong-doer of the fruits of his misdeeds,' he was to write, 'is, often, to acquire them for oneself.' Though he acknowledged some misgivings, this complemented his view that parties other than Fianna Fáil did not really win (or merit) power; they were usurpers chosen by a collective error on the part of the electorate. He once stepped down from an election platform outside the GPO to take on a heckler and he dismissed the defenders of Georgian Dublin as 'belted earls' because Desmond Guinness was among them. (Micheal Ó Morain, a Mayo solicitor who resigned as Minister for Justice as the 1970 arms crisis began, was even more dismissive of two highly respected academic observers of politics: he called them 'Trinity queers' when they questioned the party's proposals to change the electoral system.)

The mohair-suited Ministers would not have been greatly offended to have been lumped in with the liberals — a favourite target of their traditionally-minded colleagues in the 'sixties. They would have embraced the criticism as evidence of their general, all-things-to-all-men appeal. Some of their measures were, indeed, liberal and seemed to promise more radical reform. They ranged from Haughey's humane Succession Bill to Lenihan's undermining of the system of censorship and O'Malley's introduction of a scheme which he hoped would ensure that children would not be deprived of post-primary education for lack of means. O'Malley's scheme was boldly announced before his more cautious colleagues could object; Lenihan's reforms provoked so little controversy in the Dáil that he was able to move faster than he had anticipated. The bishops and some of the laity grumbled, in most cases to little avail. O'Malley was to recall how, as he put it, a reverend gentleman accompanying a delegation passed the remark: 'You will never catch us. We will always be ahead of you.' It was said jocosely but, according to O'Malley there was malice in the joke. His comment was characteristic: 'It was our divine Lord who said "suffer little children to come unto me." There will be a lot of suffering if that is the mentality that prevails in Ireland . . . Maybe some day I shall tell the tale and no better man to tell it. I shall pull no punches. Christian charity how are you.' McQuaid and Cornelius Lucey, the bishop of Cork, took exception to Lenihan's censorship changes, but he believed that most of the people and many of the priests were with him: 'I just carried on with the job. We knew we were on the right track.'

If reform and state intervention were, however grudgingly, conceded in certain areas — and some of the movements which had seemed so promising in the 'sixties just petered out — there were important sticking points: for the bishops it was divorce and for the party the constitutional claim to control over the whole island. An all-party committee, under Colley's chairmanship and on which Lemass was to serve after his resignation as Taoiseach, suggested changes in both areas. Divorce would have been permitted where people were married in the rites of a Church which did not forbid divorce. The territorial claim would have been replaced by a simple statement of the aspiration to unity. Conway, McQuaid and Lucey objected immediately to any relaxation of the ban on divorce: if it were allowed to people of one religion, everyone else would want it. And to such members of the party as Boland, any diminution of the territorial claim was little short of treachery, although Lemass had already recognised the Northern state to the extent that he was prepared to meet its Prime Minister, Terence O'Neill, and the Lemass-O'Neill meetings, about which we shall have more to say, provoked little or no controversy in the party. The all-party committee's recommendations stood no chance of success and were soon forgotten.

The party's opponents and some commentators had already begun to suspect what one of them described as a whiff of corruption and more than a hint of arrogance in the government's handling of affairs. Two attempts to change the electoral system were widely (and, possibly, wrongly) interpreted as part of a campaign to ensure that the party stayed in power forever. Corruption was believed to take the form of abuse of the planning laws, with inside information helping some politicians and many of their friends to gain advantages denied to others. Colley, in a speech made in the mid-'sixties, spoke of low standards in high places, reflecting the unease which its new reputation provoked in a section of the party; but he never got round to saying precisely what he had in mind. Blaney met the challenge to Taca in his usual fashion – head-on. At an ard-fheis where almost every other speaker had been critical of the organisation, he brilliantly turned their argument on its head. The essence of the popular complaint was that (in Boland's words) Fianna Fáil was no longer the small man's party – and Taca was the most blatant indicator of this change. Blaney's reply could be summarised

WHO IS DE VALERA ?

CLARE - ABU,

AND

DE VALERA ABU.

Of American-Irish Spanish race
DE VALERA spat in England's face,
The gap of danger's still his place
To lead historic Clare's Dragoons.

Viva la for Ireland's wrong !
Viva la for Ireland's right !
Viva la in Sinn Fein throng,
For a Spanish steed and sabre bright !

DE VALERA is 34 years of age.   In Rockwell College distinguished as
an Athlete and Scholar.   Renowned as Professor in Blackrock College.
Prominent worker for Irish Language.   For further particulars apply to
the British Army, which made his acquaintance during Easter Week

UP IRELAND !

Published for the Candidate by his Authorised Election Agent, H. O'B. Moran, Solicitor
Limerick, and Printed and Published at the CHAMPION Works, Ennis.

One of the posters that introduced de Valera to the electors of Clare in 1917.

De Valera in Lourdes in old age (*above*) and standing head and shoulders above the crowd at a political meeting in Clare (*right*).

Two of the 'old team' who vied for the leadership as the de Valera era drew to a close. Seán Lemass (*left*) and Seán MacEntee were fundamentally opposed on a number of social and economic issues. Lemass's succession to the leadership led to something approaching a revolution in Irish life.

The Boss. Charles J. Haughey has been the most controversial and enigmatic figure in the party in recent times. These pictures show him addressing an after-mass meeting during the East Galway by-election (*above left*), at the unveiling of the de Valera memorial in Ennis (*left*), delivering his presidential address at the 1980 ard-fheis (*above*) and sharing a joke with his close adviser and press officer, P. J. Mara (*right*).

The Haughey years have been dominated by a running battle between those loyal to the leadership and those who have never fully accepted Haughey's authority. Jack Lynch has never concealed his dislike for Haughey, a point underlined by the photograph (*top left*) taken at the 1979 ard-fheis, a few months before Lynch's resignation. The communication gap operated from the top down. Six years later, at the 1985 ard-fheis, Mary Harney seems less than riveted by the conversation of Haughey loyalist Seán Doherty (*left*). Meanwhile, the running battle over Haughey's leadership led to no less than three heaves against him. The photograph (*above*) shows the scene just before the parliamentary party meeting of 25 February 1982, the occasion of Des O'Malley's abortive challenge.

Haughey supporters demonstrating their loyalty in vociferous style outside party headquarters in Upper Mount Street in January 1983, on the occasion of the last attempt to oust Haughey from the party leadership.

Albert Reynolds and friend.

thus: it had, indeed, been the small man's party and many of those who were well-off today didn't have an arse to their pants when it began. It was thanks to the party that they had made good. And what they were doing in contributing to Taca was no more than a sign that they recognised this. If the delegates wanted a great party, and they did, they should not discourage any form of support. Taca, the party and the country would go on to greater things. As he ended, an old stager at ard-fheiseanna whispered in my ear: 'By Jasus, he has them in the palm of his hand.' And he had. But Taca had proved to be an embarrassment; it was to fade into the background and was quietly replaced by more subtle — at any rate, less ostentatious — forms of fund-raising, but not before some of its members made a spectral appearance during the arms crisis.

Boland may have been in a minority when he lamented the transformation of the small man's party; the shift of emphasis from rural to urban concerns was more widely and more publicly resented. Paddy Smith's resignation as Minister for Agriculture reflected his personal dissatisfaction with the importance Lemass attached to winning agreements with the trade unions. In the mid-'sixties, the two major farmers' organisations, the National Farmers' Association and the Irish Creamery Milk Suppliers' Association, embarked on a nationwide campaign to draw attention to the poor living standards and declining political influence of the agricultural community. Lemass and Haughey, who had succeeded Smith, identified them as the spokesmen of better-off farmers, old relics of Fine Gael in opposition to Fianna Fáil's conduct of the economic war. 'This is a small group of ambitious men', said Lemass, 'who want us to forego our responsibility for agricultural policy.' Farmers, drawing on the example of their French colleagues, marched on Dublin, blocked cities with their machinery, laid siege to the Department of Agriculture, delayed the payment of rates and went to jail. The N.F.A. president Rickard Deasy, whose father was one of

Lemass's adversaries twenty years earlier, turned to his followers as they trudged past Baldonnel on their way to Dublin and, pointing his stick at the empty Potez factory, one of the few failures in the programme of industrialisation, shouted: 'Take a good look, boys, that's the nearest you'll ever get to a million pounds.'

The farmers' campaign was at its most intense in the autumn of 1966, when Lemass decided to retire. The Taoiseach had seldom been ill during his period in office, but the Anglo-Irish negotiations of 1965 — they had been going on since the rejection of Britain's application to join the EEC — were particularly tiring and, with preparation for free trade now well in hand, he decided that the increasingly heavy demands of leadership should be met by a younger man. The first of his cabinet colleagues to whom he confided his decision was Jack Lynch, then Minister for Finance and the man to whom he had entrusted his own Department, Industry and Commerce, when he became Taoiseach. Lynch did not belong to any of the factions that had begun to develop in the 'sixties. He shared neither the flamboyance of the men in the mohair suits nor the dour traditionalism of Boland and Blaney. He had, however, commanded the respect of de Valera, as his assistant in opposition and a parliamentary secretary in the government of the early 'fifties; and when he came to share Lemass's vision he wholeheartedly embraced the programme of modernisation, continuing in Industry and Commerce the work that Lemass had begun, dismantling protection to make way for free trade.

Now, several months before the public announcement of his decision, Lemass told Lynch that he would like him to take over the leadership. Lynch's first reaction was self-deprecatory: taking up a position held only by Lemass and de Valera, two men whose places in history were already secure, seemed like realising an ambition he had never dared acknowledge. But, though Lemass was to take no part in the events that followed his announcement, Lynch was not in any doubt about his retiring leader's wishes: 'Lemass' he was to say, 'put his raddle-mark on me early on.'

Though the party had some warning of imminent change, Lemass's announcement threw his parliamentary colleagues into a state of confusion. Michael Mills wrote in the *Irish Press* of his probable departure a week before the formal announcement was made. The story was vigorously denied and there was some pressure on Mills to retract it. Then Colley, who was on government business in the United States, was informed by Lemass of a major development about to take place. The implication was clear — if Colley wanted to be considered for the leadership, he should return immediately. As notices went up in the party rooms convening a special meeting of the parliamentary group, the truth dawned even on those who had most vehemently denied the *Irish Press* report as wild and unsubstantiated rumour. The reason for the party's alarm was obvious: not only was there no pre-ordained successor, members were uncertain about the procedure to be adopted. The party had never had to face — or even consider facing — a contest for the leadership before. There simply was no machinery to hand. Senators, it was eventually decided, should be excluded from the electoral process, since it was the Dáil that elected the Taoiseach and, in this case as in 1979, Fianna Fáil was essentially choosing a Taoiseach. Intense lobbying of the party's 71 deputies began. The three most likely candidates, Lynch, Haughey and Colley, who had returned post haste from America, were called to the Taoiseach's office to be told formally of Lemass's decision. There was support in the party for all three and at their meeting Lemass did not express a preference. Donogh O'Malley took on the role of Haughey's campaign manager; Jim Gibbons, who was Haughey's parliamentary secretary in Finance, acted for Colley. Boland, who seemed at first to favour Aiken as a survivor of the 'old team', backed Blaney, when it became obvious that Aiken preferred Colley whom he, too, had urged home when it appeared that a contest was imminent. It looked then as though there would be a three-way contest between Haughey, Colley and Blaney: Haughey with the support of some Dublin deputies and financially influential friends; Blaney assisted by Boland's potent organisational ability and a batch of rural TDs; Colley favoured by what remained of the old guard and people who could best be described as middle-of-the-road. As worries increased about the effect on the party of a bitter contest between the three, O'Malley privately confessed that he thought Colley most likely to succeed while Blaney was convinced that his band-wagon was gaining momentum by the hour. With time running out and conflict threatening, three deputations composed largely, but not exclusively, of Munster men called on Lynch in his office. They included such seasoned campaigners as Seán Ormonde of Waterford, Tom McEllistrim of Kerry and Martin Corry of Cork, who emphasised the need for continuity and stability and argued that Lynch alone could provide both. 'You're next,' they told him and Lemass, on hearing reports of the movements in Leinster House, added his voice to the demand that had suddenly come from all sides: 'You'll have to go.' Lynch took time off to consult his wife, Maureen, before agreeing; but with his agreement to run, the outcome was in no doubt. On Lenihan's advice, Haughey and Blaney withdrew — Blaney to claim the role of king-maker — and Colley provided no more than token opposition: the voting was 52 to 19. Almost as a symbol of the party's unpreparedness for a contest, the votes were collected for counting in a shoe box, which the chief whip, Michael Carty, had picked up in a shop on the advice of Hetty Behan, the canny Kildare woman who for decades organised the party in Leinster House.

Fianna Fáil had come to be seen publicly as a party of many factions: groups attached to potential or aspiring leaders whose attractions often had less to do with politics and ideology than with personal and professional considerations — friendship, local or regional loyalty, estimations of competence and vote-getting ability. The public view of the 1966 contest was that it had really been between Colley, as the clean-cut, Irish-speaking representative of old values, and Haughey, as the high-flying spokesman of business and financial interests. If neither had proved successful, then what they had been engaged in could be regarded as a rehearsal for the real struggle, which had merely been postponed. Haughey had made a tactical retreat on the assumption that Lynch would accept the role of caretaker and that his reign would be short. Colley had forced a vote to demonstrate the seriousness of his intentions and to ensure that there would be a vote next time round when his real opponent was in the field. Blaney and Boland waited with some impatience in the wings.

Lynch lent some credence to the notion that he regarded himself as a caretaker in office when he spoke, after his election, of being a compromise candidate. It was an expression which he bitterly regretted using and, if it were taken to mean that he intended to relinquish control before too long, was completely misleading. He was to lead the party for almost twice as long as Lemass and with greater electoral success than de Valera; in retrospect, he was convinced that at all times he enjoyed the support of the vast majority of the party's members, throughout the country and in the Oireachtas. He certainly exercised a magnetic electoral appeal and, as the opinion polls showed, was never less than overwhelmingly endorsed by the party's supporters. Why this should have been is only partly explained by those who claim that Lynch reaped the benefits of Lemass's revolution, for Lemass himself was not given an overall majority in either of his elections. Nor can it be attributed to the weakness or ineptitude of the opposition: Labour mounted a powerful challenge in 1969 and in 1973, after the arms crisis had set the party's ghosts and factions on the march, Fianna Fáil was only narrowly defeated by a Coalition whose ability was acknowledged in the phrase 'a government of all the talents.' The key to Lynch's success with the electorate was suggested by two writers, who approached the subject from quite different angles, Tom Garvin, whose study of the evolution of nationalist parties I have already quoted, and Eamon Dunphy, who comments on soccer and television in the *Sunday Tribune*. Garvin, in an essay on the party since the 'sixties, refers to Lynch as 'a very unfanatical politician, with a markedly consensual style'. Dunphy, writing after the 1984 All-Ireland hurling final in Thurles, where Lynch was given a standing ovation by the crowd, remarks on the ordinariness of the man as a source of extraordinary popularity. The two descriptions are complementary. Lynch's lack of fanaticism in a party which occasionally seemed to have more than its share of zealots, his consensual style among the factions that threatened to tear it apart and the ordinariness of manner which made him seem more approachable than most other leaders — all combined to attract people across the boundaries of party and tradition. Ironically, they were the very characteristics which made him unacceptable to a section within the party that still hankered after the blazing mystique and that certain view of our people which stamped Fianna Fáil and its friends with the indelible ink of history. De Valera unquestionably possessed the blazing mystique; so, too, did Lemass, though in his case only by association since he never — or hardly ever — took refuge in the vainglorious past. Lynch, who was five years old when the vainglorious past was present, might at least have had revolutionary antecedents — Colley had, Haughey married into the family, Blaney and Boland were steeped in tradition — but he didn't.

'I never believed that it was necessary to carry a gun to be a republican,' Lynch said in 1985, but he had carried a torch for de Valera — figuratively throughout his childhood and literally when, as a boy of 15, he escorted Dev through Cork during the 1932 election. Lynch grew up among nationalists in working-class Blackpool at a time when people still remembered their defence of William O'Brien, the champion of the smallholders, against the Molly Maguires – the Hibernian hooligans who were determined to run him out of politics. In Baurgorm, a few miles from Bantry, he spent the summers with his uncles on the small farm that his father, Daniel, had left to become a tailor in Cork city at the age of 16. There Lynch considered himself equally at home with people who talked local history as well as national politics while they struggled for survival on the land; his affection for and loyalty to the west was to last a lifetime, but it was through Blackpool and the GAA that he was to make his way into active politics. Encouraged by Seán Moylan, he made his first political speech on Blackpool Bridge during a by-election in 1946. By then, he had a half-dozen All-Ireland hurling and football medals to his credit, was busy building up a practice as a barrister and had turned down a chance to stand for the Dáil. Shortly afterwards, he refused to be tempted into the newly-established Clann na Poblachta but when the offer of a Fianna Fáil nomination was repeated – by a cumann which commemorated the Delaney brothers, who were murdered by the Black and Tans – he agreed to stand in the 1948 election and won the seat easily. It was a seat he held at every election from then on, heading the poll every time since 1961. Pat Magner, a Labour senator in the 'eighties, recalled how he once tried to shake Blackpool's faith in Lynch by showing around a photograph of the Taoiseach in full morning dress in the company of some oil company bosses. 'There you are now, mam,' said Magner to an old neighbour of Lynch, stepping over the basin that gathered water from her leaky roof, 'There's Jack for you.' The old woman wiped her hands on her apron, took the photograph from the Labour man and said: 'Ah, Jesus, will you look at him. Didn't he come on grand?' Where de Valera inspired dogged admiration and deep hostility in equal measure, and Lemass excited the imagination of young people on the move, Lynch won affection. Once, on a murky fair day, he arrived early in Kilmore West in Sligo and set off, without the benefit of local guidance, through the crowd. Some of us who joined the crowd suspected that, without prompting, he would be lost. A man in a peaked cap was pushed forward by his friends to meet the Taoiseach. 'John, my poor man,' Lynch said, shaking his hand, 'I heard the news. Sorry for your trouble. I couldn't get down myself but I hope the lads made it back for the funeral.' The man was a local cumann officer whose wife had died months earlier and whose family was in England. The sympathy was spontaneous.

But Lynch was as tough as he was sympathetic, as tough as you might expect a man who had won six All-Ireland medals in a row was bound to be. When he finally resigned, he was described by Liam Cosgrave, who was Taoiseach when Lynch in opposition was known as 'the real Taoiseach', as the most popular Irish politician since Daniel O'Connell. He was also the leader who, without a faction to his name or a revolutionary record behind him, met and survived the most traumatic challenge in the party's history.

8

National Aims

Charlie Haughey was one of the people who planned Jack
Lynch's triumphal tour of the country in June 1969. Kevin
Boland wrote of the election victory that followed: 'Morale
had never been higher; our enemies were confounded, a
footstool under our feet and we were invincible again.' Two
months later only de Valera's intervention prevented Boland
from resigning, the cabinet was hopelessly divided and events
were set in train which, within a year, led to the dismissal,
trial and acquittal of Haughey and Blaney who were accused
of conspiring to import arms; the resignations of Boland,
Micheal Ó Morain and a junior Minister, Paudge Brennan,
and the most damaging crisis to have stricken Irish nationalism since the Civil War.

The immediate cause of the crisis was the police siege of
the Bogside after an Apprentice Boys' march through Derry
on 12 August. Its deeper roots lay in the contradiction
between the original nationalist aim of unity and the reality
of the twenty-six county State, in the argument between
people who saw the events in the North simply as an opportunity to achieve unity and those who were convinced that
to attempt to take that opportunity would be to provoke
violence in the North and risk instability, North and South.
In Fianna Fáil, there was a yawning gap between what the
party had always maintained was its policy — indeed, its
reason for existence — and what that policy had come to
mean, between the rhetoric inspired by that certain view

95

of history and the reality of the narrowing definitions of our people. It was a gap that had been there from the moment that de Valera had told his followers that they must face facts, of which the most obvious was the existence and popular acceptance of the Free State, but it had widened over the years with the passage of every measure that was based on the equation of faith and nation and, eventually, perhaps inevitably, with the growth of prosperity: the realisation that the South at last had something to lose was as potent a force as the acknowledgment of Catholicism as the quasi-official religion of the state. These contradictions were not confined to Fianna Fáil; they applied to Irish nationalism as a whole. What was peculiar to the party was the intensity with which they were now felt as lingering doubts about the use of force re-surfaced and competing factions seized the national question as the issue which divided them.

On the morning after the siege of the Bogside began, Haughey joined Blaney and Boland at a cabinet meeting in Dublin in demanding that the Republic take a hand in the fighting. Their argument was that the Army should go into Derry or Newry or both and (this was Haughey's view) at the very least, create an international incident which would lead to intervention by the United Nations. Lynch, who found himself isolated and opposed by the most forceful and vociferous of his colleagues, maintained that even to send one soldier across the Border would be to provoke murderous assaults on the Catholic population of Belfast; and given the known strength of the Protestant forces, the Army would probably be unable to reach and would certainly be unable to defend the city's Catholics. Furthermore, any suggestion that the Republic might become involved in a conflagration would be bound to cause a withdrawal of foreign investment from the South and the resulting unemployment would add to the difficulties produced by a Border war. He finally agreed to send field hospitals to the Border, to demand immediate negotiations with Britain on the constitutional position of Northern Ireland and to call for the urgent dispatch of a UN peacekeeping force to the North.

These developments he announced in an address on television that night in which he said: 'The Irish government can no longer stand by and see innocent people injured and perhaps worse. It is obvious that the RUC is no longer accepted as an impartial police force. Neither would the employment of British troops be acceptable nor would they be likely to restore peaceful conditions — certainly not in the long term.'

The field hospitals, he was to explain years later, had two purposes: to treat people who were afraid to enter hospitals in the North and to prevent incursions by military or civilian personnel from the South 'which would compromise us all'. The call for UN intervention came to nothing, though the Foreign Minister, Paddy Hillery, was sympathetically received in New York. The Anglo-Irish discussions, when they were finally, grudgingly conceded, became part of a process which led, with many stumbles and diversions, to Sunningdale and power-sharing in the North.

But on 13 August Lynch's address was part of a series of events which had immediate as well as long-term effects. His message was passed on to the besieged Bogsiders by the Nationalist leader, Eddie McAteer, in the form in which it has entered Irish folklore: 'We will not stand idly by'. It was interpreted by some of them as a promise of rescue and by some Protestants as a threat of invasion. The Bogsiders, meanwhile, had sent their own message to sympathisers in other Catholic areas of the North: 'Take the heat off Derry'. In Belfast, it was the signal for a series of attacks, on a police station and several business premises; rioting began simultaneously in Dungannon, Coalisland, Newry and Armagh. Senior police officers took fright, imagining that what they faced was an all-out assault on the State, and twenty-four hours later the RUC, the 'B' Specials and crowds of Protestant civilians launched a counter-offensive. Terror spread through the Catholic streets as houses were set alight and shooting began: four people, including a schoolboy, were killed that night in Belfast and hundreds were injured or driven from their homes. At once, there was talk of a pogrom similar to that which had accompanied the establishment of the Northern State in the 'twenties.

Popular reaction in Dublin was predictable. Infuriated crowds took to the streets, marching on Army barracks to demand guns and on government departments to demand official intervention. The cabinet, by now in almost continuous emergency session, decided to create a fund for the relief of distress in the North and to press ahead with an international information service which would ensure that Ireland's case was widely broadcast. Boland, who was fond of quoting de Valera's statement that partition was the gravest injury that one nation could inflict upon another, considered this response pathetically inadequate. The Taoiseach, in Boland's view, was gradually making it clear that 'partition was for keeps', though in his televised address Lynch had himself invoked de Valera: 'The reunification of the national territory can provide the only permanent solution of the problem.' Shouting of treachery and betrayal, Boland stormed out of the cabinet. There was nothing for it but to resign, he said, banging the door and retreating to his office. De Valera, who had appointed him to the cabinet in the first place, heard of his intention and called him to Arus an Uachtarain. Twenty-four hours later, Boland was back among his colleagues in the government. Looking back on de Valera's speeches about 'the gravest injury,' he was to write: 'I find myself for some reason thinking of O'Connell's promise to monster meeting after monster meeting that 1843 would be Repeal year, and the aftermath of the turning back at Clontarf.' Clearly, though he was outside the range of partisan politics, the President — as we shall see — approved of the Taoiseach's actions.

Haughey and Blaney, even more clearly, did not approve. Not alone did they support Boland's contention that de Valera had never ruled out the use of force, they persisted with the argument that now was the time to use it. An assessment of the Army's strength and equipment made it quite obvious that the course of action they favoured was foolhardy: 'We had no intention of moving in,' Lynch was to say. 'We did not have the men or equipment, even if we had the desire.' But two further actions were to be agreed: the first was that Haughey, as Minister for Finance, and Jim Gibbons, the Minister for Defence, should look to the requirements of the Army, which had been starved of funds by successive governments; the second decision, formally revealed only when Haughey and others were on trial, was that men from Derry should receive training in the use of weapons with the FCA at Fort Dunree in Donegal. 'They were Irish citizens and they were entitled to join the defence forces,' Lynch was to explain. 'It was common knowledge that the Protestant militants were better equipped and better prepared than the Catholics.'

The atmosphere in which these decisions were taken was emotional, threatening and confused. With barricades thrown up around Catholic areas of Derry and Belfast, committees were hastily assembled to protect the people who lived behind them and delegations drawn from the committees of largely middle-class citizens travelled South with requests for aid, often explicitly and publicly demanding guns. The IRA, which had in the preceding years switched from military to political activity, throwing its weight behind the Civil Rights Movement in the North, was blamed for failing to defend the Catholics of Belfast; while some of its members took their place with the new defenders, and the organisation's Army Council issued what amounted to a declaration of war, people who felt vulnerable looked to Dublin for more solid reassurance. A measure of their anxiety was provided by the welcome they gave to British troops who arrived to replace the RUC and 'B' Specials in the highly nervous zones between Protestant and Catholic ghettoes.

99

Politicans of all shades, and not just the deeper shades of green, crossed the border — some for the first time — to see what was happening and offer encouragement — occasionally money, in a few cases, guns — to the defenders before returning South to report on the conditions that 'our people' were enduring. The fact that these people had been enduring the same conditions long before the Autumn of 1969 was never mentioned, and hardly anyone bothered to investigate or inquire into the conditions endured by the other section of 'our people', the Protestants in their small streets across the way. The British Home Secretary, James Callaghan, paid an equally hasty visit, made similarly comforting promises and went home with the same superficial impressions, gained from a different but no less acute angle.

The pressure was still on Lynch, though what his critics expected him to do in the aftermath of his television address and the other actions listed above was never made clear. Invasion was unthinkable and the diplomatic offensive on which Irish embassies abroad had embarked either did not work or seemed likely to take more time than the critics were prepared to allow. Conor Cruise O'Brien, who would be regarded by all but a few Fianna Fáil members as a hostile witness, identified Lynch's predicament as one of having to talk like a republican and act like a pragmatist. Lynch was a pragmatist but after August 1969 it was impossible for pragmatists to avoid controversy with republicans. O'Brien asserts that real republicans were scarce — in the cabinet, the party and the country — but

> people influenced, half-convinced, over-awed or down-right intimidated by real republicans were far from scarce. There were also one or two people to be reckoned with, who had not hitherto been suspected of more than conventional republicanism but who now saw, in the resurgence of republican passion, a new political force, capable — like other forces — of being harnessed in the service of personal ambition.

100

The positions adopted by Blaney and Boland were unambiguous and predictable. Boland recalls how, from the start of the Civil Rights Movement in the North, Blaney had begun to 'make a nuisance of himself by introducing the extraneous matter of the Six Counties into government meetings concerned with the full-time job of consolidating the party's position of pre-eminence . . . He warned of the danger and the opportunity but was regarded as a persistent and disruptive Cassandra.' As for Boland himself: 'By this time, without having the same personal knowledge of the situation on the ground but with virtually inbred knowledge that this was what Fianna Fáil had been waiting for since 1926 . . . I was almost as troublesome as Blaney.' Haughey, however, was one of those who, in O'Brien's words, had not hitherto been suspected of more than conventional republicanism. Described by Coogan as 'the epitome of the men in the mohair suits', he was noted by a close parliamentary colleague as 'never having uttered a peep at all about the North – at party meetings or anywhere else.' Boland, whose father is said to have been highly sceptical of Haughey's merits, passes over the conversion which so surprised others and simply remarks that 'the Bogside eruption immediately produced Haughey as the third member of a caucus which insisted this was our business, the moment of truth for the Fianna Fáil party, the time for the solution of the final problem, the time for which we . . . had been waiting so very patiently since 1957.' Haughey had not only become a member of the caucus, of which Blaney was clearly the leader, he also had three functions that were of crucial importance in the sequence of events which became known as the Arms Crisis: he and Blaney were members of the cabinet sub-committee on the North; with Gibbons, he was responsible for refurbishing the Army, and he alone had the task of administering the fund made available for the relief of distress in the North. In the hands of a man of fire and ice, who was both impetuous and ambitious, and in the circumstances of Autumn 1969, these functions were bound to be critical and controversial.

Boland acknowledges that there was no groundswell in the party favouring action along the lines proposed by the cabinet caucus — a significant admission — and Lynch, having resisted the first wave of pressure, was strengthened by the support of Colley's middle-of-the-road faction and the encouragement of Hillery, whose fierce animosity towards the caucus was to be made public in a shouting-match with Boland during an ard-fheis debate. By September, Lynch felt sufficiently sure of his ground to announce in a speech delivered in Tralee: 'The unity we seek is not something forced but a free and genuine union of those living in Ireland based on mutual respect and tolerance . . . We are not seeking to overthrow by violence the Stormont parliament or government but rather to win the agreement of a sufficient number of people in the North to an acceptable form of re-unification.' The continuing resistance of the caucus to this pacific approach was bluntly expressed by Blaney less than three months later in a speech made in The Golden Grill in Letterkenny. Fair enough, the ideal way of ending partition was by peaceful means, but — and it was a major 'but' which, many thought, would have earned his dismissal — 'no-one has the right to assert that force is ruled out.' In the event, all it provoked was a reprimand from a Taoiseach to whose reprimands Blaney was insultingly indifferent — proof that, though there was no groundswell in its favour, the caucus was still too powerful to be dealt with. There was also in the air the notion — fanciful and foolish, as it turned out — that what Blaney was doing in Letterkenny was merely giving voice to long-dormant views for the benefit of his constituents: a scrap of crude and fuzzy nationalist rhetoric. Far from it, he was justifying a series of actions that he had already initiated; and the justification was to become the cause at the centre of his whole political career.

The autumn of 1969 provided fertile ground — and luxuriant

cover — for conspiratorial politics, whether designed to hijack the party or to subvert the state, or to achieve both ambitions at once. Where, in the middle years of the decade, it was considered fashionable to have go-getting speculators at your elbow, it now became the done thing to be found in the company of entertaining revolutionaries, some of whom were obliging enough to exaggerate or even to invent patriotic exploits so as to give their hosts the impression that they, too, were part of the esoteric world of intrigue. Some of them did, in a way, become part of this world by contributing funds to The Cause or The Organisation. Others for a time became immersed in the rich fantasy of vicarious involvement. At about this time Donal Foley, who was news editor of the *Irish Times*, asked Cathal Goulding, who was Chief of Staff of the IRA, how the IRA managed to keep tabs on its members. Did they carry membership cards or, as of old, letters of resignation in their pockets? 'Well, now,' said Goulding, 'it's like this. Do you think, Donal, that you're a member of the IRA?' Foley confessed that he didn't. 'Well, then,' said Goulding, 'you're not.' But in Belfast recruits to the IRA were joining in greater numbers than at any time since the 'twenties, among them men who had left the organisation when it had shifted its focus of attention from military to political affairs. And in Dublin a report presented to the cabinet claimed that IRA leaders — Goulding was mentioned specifically — had had a meeting with Haughey.

The first published report of a conspiracy in which members of the government were said to have been involved appeared in the *United Irishman* within three months of the meeting with Haughey. By this time, the IRA was on the verge of the split which produced Official and Provisional movements (that came in December) and those who took the Official side were blaming Fianna Fáil for what amounted to the establishment of the Provisional IRA. The report in the *United Irishman*, the newspaper of the republican movement, embracing the IRA and Sinn Féin, was accompanied by a set of photographs beneath which were the following captions: 'Blaney – he knows', 'Haughey – he knows', Boland – he knows', 'Lynch – can he not know?' At this point it has to be made clear that the official political and legal conclusion to the Arms Crisis (meaning the whole affair and not the alleged conspiracy) was: Blaney and Haughey were dismissed from the government; Boland resigned because, he said, Ministers had been placed under Special Branch surveillance; Ó Morain resigned at Lynch's request because of ill-health; Paudge Brennan, a junior Minister, resigned in sympathy with Boland. Blaney and Haughey, with John Kelly, a militant Belfast republican, Jim Kelly, lately resigned from the Army, and Albert Luykx, a businessman who was friendly with several Ministers, were accused of conspiring to import arms illegally. A district justice found that Blaney had no case to answer; a jury in the High Court acquitted Haughey, Luykx and the Kellys. An investigation later by the Dáil's Committee of Public Accounts revealed that £76,000 of the £100,000 voted for the relief of distress in the North was missing.

The report in the *United Irishman*, which was written by the paper's editor, Seamus Ó Tuathail, claimed that attempts were being made by Blaney, Haughey and Boland to gain control of the Civil Rights Movement and spoke of promises of guns, as well as help with printing and propaganda, for people in the North. It asked: 'Is this plan an official government – or an official Fianna Fáil – plan? How much of this work has been financed by government money?' What provoked these questions were: the chance discovery that Seamus Brady, a close associate of Blaney, was engaged in the preparation of propaganda material; a revealing remark made by Brady about Haughey's intentions; offers and suggestions made by some of Haughey's associates to Goulding, and the activities of Jim Kelly in border areas, particularly in his native county, Cavan, and in Monaghan.

Ó Tuathail, quite by accident, discovered that Brady, a former journalist of wide experience who was employed by

Blaney on departmental work and by the government in its recently initiated propaganda campaign, was engaged in the production of a newspaper called *The Voice of the North* and had written a booklet entitled *Terror in Northern Ireland*, the first purporting to be a publication of a Monaghan civil rights group, the second being circulated without imprint as if it were produced in the North. Both advanced the Blaney-Boland-Haughey line and *The Voice of the North* was financed by funds from the Department of the Taoiseach until Lynch put a stop to it. Ó Tuathail got into conversation with Brady, who made it clear that leading Fianna Fáil men believed the events of August were going to be repeated and that, this time, there was going to be a military solution. This seemed to bear out the suspicions raised by the offers made to Goulding, who had been called hurriedly to London to meet an Irishman with close party connections for a discussion about providing arms for the North. The meeting took place in a priest's house in Kilburn, where Goulding was asked how much he thought it would cost to provide sufficient arms to protect Catholic areas. His estimate was that £50,000 would be needed. The money could be raised, he was told, by sympathisers and friends. The information was also passed on to a meeting of people involved in defence committees, including members of the IRA from North and South, by Jim Kelly. This meeting, held at Bailieboro, Co. Cavan, on 4 October, was told that £50,000 would be made available for the purchase of arms. According to Kelly, as quoted by Vincent Browne in *Magill* magazine (May 1980), it was 'the genesis of the plan to import arms'.

Ó Tuathail's report was wrong about Boland when it implied that he knew of arms deals, though the openness of Kelly's activities, as a member of Army intelligence, may have suggested a plan that had at least covert official support. The same implication is contained in the question: 'Lynch — can he not know?' It would appear that, although Lynch was told of the importation of a small quantity of arms around October 1969, he did not learn of the alleged conspiracy which was to be the subject of the trial and the reason for the dismissal of Blaney and Haughey until April 1970. He specifically denied Ministerial involvement in a plot within days of the publication of the report in the *United Irishman* in November 1969. And he denies the assertion in the Berry papers — diaries and other comments published in *Magill* (June 1980) — that the former secretary of the Department of Justice, Peter Berry, told him on 17 October of Kelly's activities, his role in the Bailieboro meeting and the offer of £50,000 for the purchase of arms. Berry had just begun to undergo medical tests when the Taoiseach, at his request, called to see him in Mount Carmel Hospital:

> I had been given an injection and rubber tubing had been inserted through a nostril to the stomach before the Taoiseach arrived sometime after nine o'clock. There were two doctors and two nurses in the room and while they left to make way for the Taoiseach a nurse kept coming in and out, every couple of minutes, to syphon off liquid through the tubing. After our conversation was interrupted a couple of times the Taoiseach said petulantly: 'This is hopeless. I will get in touch with you again.' He never resumed the conversation or referred to it afterwards.

In a passage obviously written later (Berry frequently added to his diary entries) he continued:

> I did not have a 100 per cent recollection of my conversation with the Taoiseach as I was a bit muzzy and bloody from the medical tests but I am quite certain that I told him of Captain Kelly's prominent part in the Bailieboro meeting ... I remember a conjecture of the Taoiseach as to where could they possibly get [the £50,000] and my suggestion that perhaps Mr Y or Mr Z, two millionaires of the Taca Group, might put up the

the money and the Taoiseach's observation that those boys didn't give it up easily.

Still later, he recalls how Gibbons, the Minister for Defence, and Col. Michael Hefferon, the Director of Military Intelligence, contradicted each other's evidence to the Public Accounts Committee about a conversation they were supposed to have had during which Gibbons, according to Hefferon, spoke of Berry's report to the Taoiseach about the Bailieboro meeting. Gibbons said he was never told of that meeting. Berry's inference is that the information could only have come to Hefferon, via Gibbons, from Lynch.

Lynch's account of his conversation with Berry is quite different from Berry's account of it. There was no discussion of Kelly's activities or of the £50,000, but 'he told me about the discovery of a little [arms] dump in Dublin Airport. It was watched, he said, until two men came to collect it and it was taken up the Dublin mountains. The men were followed [by the gardaí]. I asked him why they did not pounce. He said the source of the information would have been obvious and would have been exterminated.' There had, indeed, been attempts to import arms, some of them ludicrously inept. One involved the IRA and another the small left-wing offshoot of the IRA, Saor Eire. They fell foul of British intelligence, one of whose operators posed as an arms dealer and turned up in Dublin, without weapons but with a request that he should be taken to see a training camp. Only the intervention of Jim Kelly prevented his being shot. The informant of whom Berry spoke to Lynch, however, was an insider — one of two men, one of whom was deeply involved with the IRA, the other attached to Saor Eire — who was providing the gardaí with detailed information about operations, supplies and activists.

Berry, who liked to be known as the grey eminence of the Department of Justice, considered himself an expert on subversion of all sorts but was particularly suspicious of movements on the left. He cast a cold eye on the eleven Ministers he served and had differences with several of them, including Haughey and Lenihan; he was to retire early, after which he unsuccessfully took action for libel (against the *Irish Times*) and for compensation which he claimed Lynch and Des O'Malley, who succeeded Ó Morain, had promised him. But he was a stickler for protocol and reported to his own Minister for whom he prepared cabinet memoranda, on the assumption that the Minister was reporting to the government. In Ó Morain's case, this was not what happened.

A gruff but amiable man, Ó Morain was upset by the reaction of some of his colleagues to the report on the Haughey-Goulding meeting and in the months that followed made few contributions to cabinet meetings. He was ill for much of the time and, according to colleagues, was frequently absent from his office. He had little stomach for the detailed and relentless demands the job made on him. Once capable of rugged stonewalling in the Dáil, during his last six months in office he seemed uncertain and confused. Lynch was adamant in his insistence that Ó Morain did not pass on the reports which, Berry maintained, had been prepared for him. Berry himself appeared to suspect that this was the case. He described Ó Morain as having been, at various times, incoherent, listless and unaware of what was being said to him. But it remained Berry's practice to report only to his Minister until, with events coming to a head in the third week of April 1970, he sought the advice of the President. According to Berry, he told de Valera: 'I have come into knowledge of matters of national concern. I am afraid that if I follow the normal course the information might not reach the government. Does my duty end with informing my Minister or am I responsible to the government by whom I am appointed?' The President advised him to speak to the Taoiseach.

Berry's information was that a plot to import several tons of arms had been uncovered. Blaney and Haughey were said to be involved. The arms had been bought by Jim Kelly in Germany and only a combination of mistakes by the plotters, sharp observation by airline officials and surveillance by the Special Branch had prevented their importation. Lynch felt betrayed, angry and, at first, reluctant to believe what he heard. He asked Berry to check his facts. 'I thought you knew about it,' Berry said, 'the Minister told me he was keeping you informed.' Lynch's sense of isolation – he was to describe it as loneliness – revived the nagging feeling that, for all his electoral popularity, he was regarded as an outsider by an important section of the party. It added to the sense of betrayal. After the June election and Haughey's role as one of his campaign organisers, he had thought that he was becoming more acceptable to the factions that opposed him. Now, it was clear that that was an illusion. Ó Morain's case, too, exemplified his problems in the party: he had already refused to take action against the Minister for Justice in spite of his obvious illness and the fact that he was continuing to run a legal practice in Mayo, because Ó Morain was one of the cabinet's veterans who had been given his first promotion by de Valera. Ó Morain, when he was finally contacted, lamely explained that he had not passed on Berry's reports to the cabinet because he could not believe that his colleagues were involved; and Jim Gibbons, when he was summoned from the Department of Defence, said that when he had asked Ó Morain about telling Lynch what was going on the senior Minister put him off with the promise that he was about to inform the Taoiseach. Lynch consulted with Colley and, virtually accusing Ó Morain of dereliction of duty, decided to ask for his resignation. (Ó Morain, who was in hospital following a collapse in the Gresham Hotel on 22 April, resigned on 4 May.)

In the meantime – on 21 April, the day after he had first spoken to him about the arms plot – Berry returned to the Taoiseach with affidavits from customs officials and the revenue commissioners which finally convinced him, as he re-read them at home in Rathgar, that drastic action was unavoidable. Next day was Budget Day; he would call Haughey and Blaney to his office in Leinster House and confront them with Berry's information. Even now he knew that he had to be sure of his ground before dismissing them and he was conscious of the fact that, whatever happened, the future of the party at least was at stake. Next morning, however, Haughey was seriously ill in hospital: according to his own story because he had fallen from a horse, a story which Lynch still refuses to accept. The Taoiseach delivered the Budget and postponed the confrontation. That delay — Lynch decided to deal with the two men together — provoked serious criticism in the Dáil when the decisions were finally announced. So did an evasive answer to a question by Liam Cosgrave, the leader of Fine Gael, about the resignation of Ó Morain.

As far as the Dáil was concerned, the parliamentary fuse was lit at four o'clock on Wednesday, 5 May, with the following exchange:

> *Cosgrave:* Can the Taoiseach say if this is the only Ministerial resignation we can expect?
> *Lynch:* I do not know what the deputy is referring to.
> *Cosgrave:* Is it only the tip of the iceberg?
> *Lynch*: Would the deputy like to enlarge on what he has in mind?
> *Cosgrave:* The Taoiseach can deal with the situation?
> *Lynch:* I can assure the deputy I am in complete control of whatever situation might arise.

Ten hours later, the night news editors of the daily papers were officially told that Haughey and Blaney had been dismissed. As he asked his questions, Cosgrave had in his pocket a piece of paper which, had he chosen to produce it to the Dáil, would almost certainly have ensured the collapse of the government.

9

The Ghosts Walk

The message on Liam Cosgrave's piece of paper was little different from the information given to the Taoiseach by the secretary of the Department of Justice. But had Cosgrave suddenly produced that information to the Dáil instead of going to the Taoiseach privately, and had that been the first the Dáil heard of the affair, the impact on the government would have been irresistible. As it was, the action taken by Lynch following Cosgrave's visit to his office on 5 May and the revelations, which began to flow next day and continued to flow for more than a year, from Dáil debates, two trials (one abortive) and an investigation by the Dáil's Committee of Public Accounts, stunned the country and shook Fianna Fáil to its foundations. Many of the party's deputies, senators and local representatives, attempting to find their way through a labyrinth of evidence, over-hung with accusations, counter-accusations and competing claims on their loyalty, ended up relying on instinct or suspended judgment on what had really happened because of the need to preserve the tattered remains of the organisation's unity and self-respect. Although the courts acquitted the accused and the committee's conclusions were vague, the general atmosphere was such that few questioned Lynch's right to dismiss Blaney and Haughey on the grounds that no hint of suspicion should attach to any member of the government. Some people still wondered if they were, even yet, only glimpsing the tip of the iceberg; they suspected that, hidden beneath

111

the carefully chosen words of lawyers and senior politicians, in the answers issuing from courtrooms and committee-rooms, there were other layers of meaning. Experienced observers of politics had to think twice and think again before deciding whether 'yea' and 'nay' meant yea and nay in statements intended to carry separate, often contradictory, messages to different audiences — inquisitors and jurors, allies and enemies, local and national constituencies and the electorate at large.

The story of the attempted importation is not easily summarised. Jim Kelly, a captain in military intelligence, considered himself a liaison officer between the cabinet's sub-committee on the North, specifically Blaney and Haughey, and the Northern defence committees, some of whom were clamouring for guns and saw guns, or money to pay the defenders of Catholic areas, as the most useful means of relieving distress. To acquire guns, Kelly travelled to several countries and made contact with various arms dealers. He was accompanied on some trips by Albert Luykx, who acted as interpreter, and on others by John Kelly, one of the Belfast defenders, who was also involved in separate attempts to buy arms. Jim Kelly, with the help of Luykx, eventually came to an arrangement with a German dealer, Otto Schleuter of Hamburg, for the supply of sub-machine guns, machine guns, grenades and other equipment. The Public Accounts Committee heard that £32,000 from a Dublin bank account opened under a fictitious name was used to finance the purchase of German arms. The money came from the grant-in-aid voted by the Dáil for the relief of distress in the North, a fund administered by Haughey. The intention was that the arms should be transferred from Germany to Dublin where they would be hidden in a convent before being taken to a monastery near the Border for distribution to the defence committees, many of which were now dominated by personnel who were or would soon become members of the Provisional IRA. The plan mis-fired because of problems with transport and documentation and so came to the attention of

112

Peter Berry in the Department of Justice. According to Berry, Haughey attempted to intervene and asked if the consignment could be let through on condition that it was taken immediately to the North; otherwise, it might be postponed for a month. Haughey was to deny that he had had any part in — or knowledge of — the attempted importation. He was also to deny that he knew of, or had authorised, the use of funds from the grant-in-aid for the purchase of arms. Blaney, too, denied all knowledge of, or involvement in, the plot. In court, the Kellys and Luykx put up a different defence. What they denied was that the attempted importation was illegal, and Jim Kelly said in evidence that the Ministers knew what was going on. A district court found that Blaney had no case to answer. A jury in the High Court acquitted Haughey, Luykx and the Kellys. The Public Accounts Committee found that, of the £105,000 in the fund for the relief of distess, £29,000 had been spent for that purpose, over £34,000 had been spent in Belfast for 'undetermined purposes' and more than £41,000 had not been spent on the relief of distress. There was considerable public sympathy for some of those who were involved, directly or by implication, in the affair. Jim Kelly and Michael Hefferon, his boss in military intelligence, suffered public ignominy although Kelly maintained, and Hefferon believed, that Kelly was acting on behalf of the government, or at least its Northern sub-committee, and specifically with the approval of Blaney and Haughey. Kelly also claimed that Jim Gibbons, as Minister for Defence, knew what he was doing and accused Gibbons of telling 'a tissue of lies' when he denied it. Directly contradicting Haughey's evidence in court, Gibbons, too, was the target of much vehement abuse, but Lynch, following his own investigation of the information which Berry and Cosgrave had given him, accepted Gibbons's word and promoted him to Blaney's old post in Agriculture.

May 6th was the day of the annual commemoration at Arbour Hill. As they left the spare, grey yard where they had honoured their common ancestors in the struggle for independence, most of the politicians expected and feared a general election. The news of the dismissals had exploded in their faces, igniting rumours of the government's imminent collapse. An election, in the circumstances, would have been the bloodiest since 1932 with consequences which, in the long run, might have been as serious as those of the Civil War. As they gathered in Leinster House, deputies, senators and supporters of all parties moved nervously from group to group, attempting to separate fact from rumour and, in the case of Fianna Fáil members and supporters, to gain reassurance from the factions to which they belonged. Blaney's supporters customarily occupied a large table beside the coat-stand in the members' restaurant: they and their meeting-place became known as 'the hat-rack parliament'. Anyone seen heading in that direction was immediately suspected of being a member. A senior Fine Gael man, who had favoured a more aggressive line than Cosgrave was prepared to take, found a ready audience for wild-eyed speculation about a military coup. Politicians who had always been regarded an easy-going, friendly men suddenly became distant and nervous, unwilling to be seen talking to old colleagues whom they imagined to be in a different camp. In the bars, corridors and committee rooms, people eyed each other as if they were strangers whose intentions were dubious if not hostile. A hurriedly arranged meeting of the Fianna Fáil parliamentary party was expected to produce the eruption which would topple the government and precipitate an election. Lynch steeled himself for the collision. With the support of Colley, Hillery and such senior deputies as Aiken and Padraig Faulkner of Louth, he presented the party with an outline of the reasons for the action he had taken and offered them the choice: they could support him or face an election in which they would, almost certainly, be forced out of office. As in the 'twenties, when de Valera and the 'old team' had used the prospect of their 'faithless fellows' forever holding power to convince another generation that they should join the party, the argument worked. It took less than an hour to make the choice: there would be no election. It was probably the most remarkable example of an Irish party's instinct for self-preservation overcoming its internal divisions, an example of pragmatism without parallel in the history of constitutional nationalism in Ireland. For the party was now to face the most sustained attack that had ever been made on it; one debate continued day and night for 37½ hours, and never had the contradiction between rhetoric and reality been more cruelly exposed.

Lynch's cautious, sparse and legalistic account of events did less to reassure his nervous colleagues than to frustrate those who demanded a full report on what had happened. But Boland and Blaney were thunderously vocal about the political differences that had rocked the cabinet. Boland, who complained to journalists of Gestapo-like tactics employed by one section of the government against another, was only slightly less colourful when he gave the Dáil his reasons for resigning. Remembering an old Army saying — 'If an NCO says you're drunk, you're drunk' — he told the House: 'I do not accept that it is reasonable to expect Ministers to serve under the condition that if Mr Peter Berry says you did a thing, you did it.' He accused Berry of running an organisation to keep Ministers under surveillance, threw in the rumour that the British secret service might have had a hand in the concoction of a story 'which lacks nothing except the introduction of a beautiful blonde or two' and suggested that the source of the information made available to Lynch and Cosgrave was tainted. Unification could not be achieved by force — 'as anybody with any normal intelligence will see' — but the people in the Six Counties were now in the position that everyone else had been in before 1916 and 'it would be unpardonable for us to take any action to frustrate the efforts of our people in the Six Counties to protect their lives and property.' He objected to 'the attitude that the over-riding concern must be to retain this state and this parliament'. A twenty-six county state was not an achievement but a result of the 1922 betrayal and, while he recognised that it existed and must be worked, 'the national objective must be to get rid of two states in this country and not one.' Importing arms into the Republic was illegal but importing arms into the North was not, and it was not the business of the authorities in the Republic to interfere with it; co-operation with the security forces in the North was intolerable.

Haughey, who was ill, had already issued his denial of involvement in the plot, adding: 'I fully accept the Taoiseach's decision as I believe the unity of the Fianna Fáil party is of greater importance to the welfare of the nation than my political career.' Blaney's denial of involvement was even more explicit: 'I have run no guns. I have procured no guns. I have provided no money to buy guns and anybody who says otherwise is not telling the truth.' (In November, 1971 he was to say: 'Give [the Provisional IRA] aid and money and anything else that might be useful to them. Let the people who are carrying on the struggle in Northern Ireland know that you are with them.') Where Boland had been sarcastic, Blaney was direct. He'd been born while his father was under sentence of death. As a child, he'd been kicked out of his cot 'by one of the force of the then alleged nation'; he and his family had been terrified by (the Free State) military and police, 'fellows who were as often drunk as they were sober, perhaps because, having sold out their republican principles, they had to drown their shame in liquor.' As a boy he had been 'kicked by a Blueshirt black and blue on my way home from school' for sporting a tricolour. Now he derived 'great strength from my breeding' and accused the Fine Gael leaders of 'following in the footsteps of their predecessors in 1925, who sold out on the Border question and handed over almost half a million of our people, against those people's expressed wish and against the expressed wish

116

of the majority of all the people of this island . . . to the domination of the Orange junta in Stormont.'

If Boland attacked Lynch by accusing Berry, Blaney attacked him by accusing Fine Gael. He denied he had ever advocated the use of force to achieve unity but insisted 'I do not retreat from what I have done to help and encourage our people who were being brutally assaulted.' He denied there was a split in Fianna Fáil but explained his refusal to resign when Lynch had demanded his resignation: 'With no disrespect to the Taoiseach or to the government, and with sadness so far as the President of the country is concerned, I refused to resign because I believe that by doing so, in view of the extremely delicate situation in the Six Counties, I would be aiding, perhaps causing, something that would result in some explosion about which we might be very sorry in the future.' He did not say what explosion was likely but returned to the theme of loyalty with a declaration on his own behalf and on behalf of Haughey and Ó Morain: 'There is no question about our allegiance to the leadership of Fianna Fáil. . . . Fianna Fáil and their continuance is synonymous with the advancement of this country and the ultimate bringing about of unity and the betterment of all our people.'

This speech caused Maurice Dockrell, a normally reticent Fine Gael deputy, to comment on 'that strange sad bitterness that came out' when Blaney spoke: 'he forces his mind into the past and lashes himself with pity.' But Blaney was not alone in calling up the ghosts of the Civil War or of more recent conflict. Opposition deputies, too, dredged the murky depths as when Seán Treacy of Labour recalled the 'many republicans sent to their death by the rope and bullet and many more thousands incarcerated . . . by the so-called Republican Party' and added: 'There would not be a God if this did not boomerang on them.' However, attention was fixed firmly on Boland and Blaney and on speeches which, as Conor Cruise O'Brien of Labour said, had already fallen on attentive and fanatical ears in the North: 'Those who rouse up passion, the Paisleys or the Blaneys, play into each other's hands and they confirm one another's prophecies of woe.'

Prophecies of woe in Fianna Fáil rose relentlessly from the Fine Gael and Labour benches. As the Taoiseach lost his mantle of infallibility, said Noel Browne, the polarisation, pro-Lynch and pro-Haughey, must become exacerbated and intensified and could lead only to growing inefficiency until they found it impossible to unite. David Thornley, a respected historian argued: 'The history of Fianna Fáil has finally caught up with it and broken it.' Tom O'Higgins, who fought two Presidential elections and was to become Chief Justice, said: 'It was a hopeless effort to mix two brands and two ideals, to mix the captive republicanism of the past with the modern, mohaired approach. This mixing of water and wine did not produce a good bottle.' Justin Keating put it another way: 'National unity is important to (Fianna Fáil) but as a substitute, as a sort of lightning conductor for the things they know they cannot have . . . Republicanism in song and in language without republicanism in money is basically hollow.'

Knowing that, for the time being at least, their majority was secure, the Fianna Fáil men doggedly persisted in their assertion that there was no split, no crisis, no reason for alarm and, above all, no question of their loyalty. 'This is something that people may find it very difficult to understand,' said Paudge Brennan, explaining his resignation. 'So long as the party remains the republican party that it is and so long as it holds dear the aims of its founders . . . then the Taoiseach, the members of his government and the parliamentary party will have my support. None of them need have any doubt whatsoever on that score.' Some sought other targets. 'Chub' O'Connor of Kerry remembered the civil war atrocity at Ballyseedy and Joe Dowling of Dublin accused Cosgrave's informant: 'it would appear that there is a double agent in the police . . . How much was that man paid for the information? . . . Whoever was the renegade or traitor who sold the information must be discovered.' The debate ground on, now with passionate intensity and occasionally with elements of farce. A Fine Gael backbencher, somewhat the worse for wear, would wake up now and then and shout 'hear, hear' at inappropriate moments. Oliver J. Flanagan, a Knight of St Columbanus, complained that he had been called a communist, which was too much for Joe Leneghan of Fianna Fáil who hauled himself to his feet, muttered 'Jasus, I could stand anything but that' and left. Someone recalled the advice of a former Fine Gael leader, James Dillon: 'Beware of entering politics lest your soul be damned.' A Labour deputy claimed that Fianna Fáil men had set about frightening a colleague's constituents by asking them 'Would you like to see your parish priest in chains?' And an elderly gentleman moaned 'Up the Republic' before sliding off his seat and out of sight.

There were reports of growing support for Blaney and Haughey in and around their constituencies. Eddie McAteer, the Nationalist leader, said in Derry: 'My party remains committed to the Lynch peace line but this does not mean that we will meekly bow down like sheep for summer slaughter. The screeching doves may well remember that Neil Blaney stood beside us in our hour of need and is still willing to sacrifice a bright political future to help his fellow Ulstermen. If the midnight knock comes to our door, would not the gentlest of us love the feeling of security which a pike in the thatch can give?' In Donegal, preparations were being made to give the sacked Minister a hero's welcome. 'Bonfires blaze for Blaney,' was the headline in the *Evening Herald* and the same paper quoted Haughey's election agent, Pat O'Connor, announcing that the people of Dublin north-east were in rebellious mood. Clearly, the pledges of loyalty to the leadership and the declarations of party unity were seen by the Blaneyites and Haugheyites as empty formulae, intended to gloss over their differences with Lynch, not to eliminate them. 'Yes' in this case did not mean acquiescence or agreement; the pike in the thatch and the bonfires across the Border spoke more eloquently than denials in the Dáil. But, for Lynch, there was no going back on the decisions that had been taken and when he said 'I want to protect economic growth and progress, I do not want it prejudiced and I shall do everything in my power to ensure that violence on this or on the other side of the Border will not prejudice it' he was making the most significant point of the debate. Not only was violence futile and talk of unity misleading, the relative prosperity which the Republic had achieved was now a major consideration, along with the protection of the State and of institutions that Fianna Fáil, more than any other party, had helped to shape. There could be no retreat: time and again during the next year, he was to ensure that the party faced the choice between support for him and a risky election. For Boland and Blaney, it was a bitter choice but they supported the government and the party until Boland quit to establish his own, short-lived republican group, Aontacht Éireann, and Blaney was finally expelled. Haughey, who was not present for the May debate, took his place on the back benches and slowly, assiduously, resumed his quest for power.

The arms crisis had been caused by two things: the existence in the party of competing factions which were prepared to seize any issue as a vehicle for their ambitions and the party's failure to arrive at any clear definition of its first national aim and how it might be received. The genesis of the factions has already been described. The arms crisis dramatised their differences on the national question, with enthusiastic applause for Boland and Blaney in the Dáil indicating the strength of opposition to the leadership. The most innocent explanation of what had happened was that, to the habits of government by wink and nod and the mohair men's predilection for cutting corners, had been added the conviction of some members of one faction that, come what may, they and their associates could be kept beyond the reach of law; but they had grown careless over the years and were caught, or trapped, as much by their own assumptions of invulnerability as by the vigilance or cunning of their opponents. Lynch was accused of having delayed too long the dismissals that eventually became the focal point of the crisis, the implication being that he was prepared to turn a blind eye to the activities of his colleagues. This was a suspicion harboured by Berry (it was the reason he contacted de Valera) and by some senior officers in the gardaí (it was probably what caused one of them to send the message to Cosgrave). The theory is seriously flawed: Lynch felt that he was the principal target of his factional opponents and recognised that confrontation with them was inevitable. He delayed taking action so that he could be sure of his ground, as a lawyer and as a politician, when he tackled them. He was enraged by Berry's contact with de Valera and saw no reason whatever for confiding in a man who obviously suspected that he, the Taoiseach, was somehow involved. And, at the most basic level, it would be completely unrealistic for anyone in his position to imagine that Ministerial involvement in a plot to import arms, already suspected by several people outside the government, would go unnoticed. Lynch, whose lack of fanaticism has already been noted, was not a man to take risks; and he had now, if only by association with Colley, acquired a faction of his own.

The party's internal stresses would not have surfaced so dramatically — and might not have had such a long-term effect — had it defined precisely what it meant by its first aim: 'To secure the unity and independence of Ireland as a republic.' But an unwillingness to accept that there might be any question as to what it meant, and the refusal to acknowledge the reality of policy changes by its leaders, prevented a debate from which an agreed definition might have sprung. Indeed, what is most surprising about the changes in policy during the periods in which de Valera and Lemass led the party is how little fuss they caused and how readily they were accepted by its members, not to mention the electorate. Of course, they blew hot or cold, depending on whether they were in government or opposition — just as Haughey, in the 'eighties, took on a deeper shade of green when he was out of office but in office made much of the unique relationship between Ireland and Britain — but both de Valera and Lemass displayed a pragmatism which must have been the envy of their forever suspect 'faithless fellows' in Fine Gael. De Valera in particular could be cited in support of almost any suggestion to resolve the national question. He was not even prepared to dismiss out of hand the idea that Ireland, united, might return to the British Commonwealth: 'A conference would be necessary to settle this question,' he said, 'and at such a conference the question of a new relationship with Britain would have to be settled.' Between the 'twenties and the 'fifties, he moved gradually from a position of insisting that force should not be ruled out to one of acknowledging that nobody could promise unity and, essentially, asserted — as Lynch did — that the defence and welfare of the State they controlled must be the first task of Irish politicians. He suggested, in the 'twenties, that counties might be permitted to make their separate decisions as to what state they joined; in the 'fifties, he advocated federation. Addressing the Unionists obliquely, which was the only way he ever addressed them, he announced that the South had no intention of changing to accommodate their views because their position 'fundamentally is not as just as our position is'. He was at the time (the late 'forties) toying with the notion of repatriation: 'If you don't want to be Irish, we are prepared to let you go and compensate you.' But he had already, in the 1938 Anglo-Irish negotiations, made it clear that he was opposed to the use of force by Britain to compel the Unionists to enter any arrangement against their wishes. A year later he was telling the Senate: 'Not tomorrow, for the sake of a united Ireland [would I] give up the policy of trying to make this a really Irish Ireland — not by any means.' He was, however, convinced that the history, tradition and culture of 'the historic Irish nation' could not fail to attract the Unionists; and while he was opposed to their coercion what he demanded of Britain was a public declaration of commitment to unity, a cessation of military coercion of the Border nationalists and the ending of British support for partition. By the time he fought his last election, in 1957, he had come to the conclusion that '[if] we make sure that this five-sixths is made really Irish, we will have the preservation of the Irish nation in our hands; time will settle the other thing.' And after he had retired from party politics he told the *New York Times*: 'France was France without Alsace and Lorraine . . . Ireland is Ireland without the North.' He had reached the point where he reminded Boland of Daniel O'Connell.

The course charted by de Valera was erratic, perhaps because it served the needs of the party as he saw them rather than any broader vision of unity. He had been prepared to countenance the use of force (in theory, at least) when what the party needed was the support of people who had been involved in the Civil War. In government, however, he negotiated the step-by-step removal of the 'trappings of Empire' and surprised British politicians and officials with his realism. When the IRA launched their offensive against Britain during the Second World War, de Valera and Gerry Boland, who was Minister for Justice, met the challenge head-on: tribunals imposed death sentences which were carried out without delay, prisoners died on hunger-strike, men were shot in battles with the gardaí. Some of the dead and scores of internees were one-time comrades of the old warriors. The action taken against them was necessary to ensure the security of the State, the stability of the government and the survival of the party. The IRA's determined anglophobia — and support for Germany, among its most militant activities — probably influenced de Valera's view that 'for a divided people to fling itself into this war would be to commit suicide'. It did not take from his courageous and scrupulous

123

adherence to neutrality, a policy which had been presaged by his brave efforts at the League of Nations to prevent the war. After the war and the declaration of a Republic by the first inter-party government, a declaration which Fianna Fáil supported with some misgivings, de Valera embarked on a world tour during which he attempted to retrieve his position as the voice of Irish nationalism, but by now it was clear that unity was not going to be achieved in his time and the party's defeat in 1954 reinforced Lemass's argument that other matters had caught the attention of the electorate. De Valera duly changed course: time would settle 'the other thing'.

De Valera's shifts of emphasis indicate a degree of flexibility with which he was seldom credited during his lifetime. He may well come to be seen as a believer in two things — cultural nationalism and the power of the party. But the idea that the history, traditions and culture of 'the historic Irish nation' would prove irresistibly attractive to the Unionists was, in marked contrast to the moderation of his eventual attitude to unity, incredibly naive. The party had been shaped, not by its vision of a historic Irish nation, but by its reduction of that vision to twenty-six counties, Catholic orthodoxy and a couple of slogans: 'Up the Republic' and 'Up Dev'. It was not a rich inheritance.

It was an inheritance that many members of the party chose to accept in the 'seventies and 'eighties in preference to any serious, critical examination of what de Valera said or did. As in the past, it was what they wanted to believe about him that mattered.

Lemass chose to say little about the first national aim but what he did say was different, in tone and content, from de Valera's earlier utterances and far removed from what de Valera was popularly supposed to have believed. The fact that he said so little was in itself significant: he took the view that attention should be focused on the Republic and the use of such independence as had been achieved to create a society which might prove attractive to the people of the North,

both nationalist and unionist. High unemployment and ener-
vating emigration were no advertisements for unity, an argument he used with considerable effect in his internal debate
with de Valera, MacEntee and Aiken about the urgent need
for economic development. If his meeting with Terence
O'Neill, in January 1965, represented the first — and most
widely acclaimed — recognition of the need for detente with
the North, his statement that unity meant bringing people
together and was not a matter of territorial acquisition introduced a note of realism which, at the time, verged on the
revolutionary. Because unity had been seen as an acquisitive
matter it had also become impersonal, a question of recover-
ing the Fourth Green Field almost without reference to the
people who lived in it and certainly with scant regard for the
wishes of those who had no desire to become part of an all-
Ireland republic. Now, Lemass was suddenly broadening the
notion of unity and, by acknowledging the need to bring
people together, accepting a gradualist approach. He was,
in fact, taking de Valera at his word — or, at any rate, at his
final word to the Oireachtas: it would be a long haul. This
raised the question of the constitutional claim, implicit in
articles two and three, the first of which defined the national
territory as the whole island, the second of which defined the
area over which the government had jurisdiction, 'pending
the re-integration of the national territory' and without prejudice to the government's right, as established by the constitution, to exercise jurisdiction over the whole. It raised
other questions, too, about the nature of a State which had
been so clearly designed to meet the demands of its Catholic
majority. Both sets of questions were examined by the
all-party committee chaired by Colley on which Lemass
served after he had resigned as leader and Taoiseach. The
committee's report, published in 1967, included recommendations on the special position of the Catholic Church and,
as already described, on divorce and the replacement of article
three. The special position of the Catholic Church was even-

125

tually removed by referendum; the recommendations on divorce and article three — an aspiration to unity 'in harmony and brotherly affection between all Irishmen' was to replace the claim — were dropped because of objections by the bishops and the party.

Though Lemass's adoption of gradualism did not lead to its logical constitutional conclusion, it proved acceptable as a policy — there were no immediate objections to that — and the policy was followed by Lynch who continued the series of meetings with O'Neill and, from 1969 onwards, negotiated with successive British governments on the basis that the Republic had a legitimate interest in the North and sought only unity by consent. The suggestion that Lynch suddenly changed policy in 1969 was not true. Indeed, during and after the 1970 crisis, de Valera, Aiken and MacEntee gave him their approval and support. In 1973, Aiken refused to accept a Fianna Fáil nomination in Louth, the constituency he had represented throughout his parliamentary career, because he objected to Haughey's nomination by the party. MacEntee had written early in 1970 a frank admission that on the question of unity the elders had failed: 'Maybe we were too rigid in our approach, too tenacious of our point of view, too proud to temporise or placate. Whatever may have been the reason, we made no headway; so our successors must start from "square one".'

Some members of the party believed that, if only de Valera were free to speak out in 1970, he would have supported the militant point of view. In fact, he told Des O'Malley at least twice that he fully supported Lynch. O'Malley had been appointed Minister for Justice in place of Ó Morain and, as part of his new duties, accompanied judges to Arus an Uachtarain when they received their seals of office from the President. On these visits he would be asked to stay behind when the Taoiseach and the judges left. During long, private conversations in the President's study, de Valera would inquire deeply into affairs of State and developments

126

in the party. O'Malley recalls: 'He left me in no doubt at all that he was entirely in agreement with and supportive of Jack Lynch. This applied both to his Northern policy generally and to the action he had taken within the party.'

10

Ireland's Tory Party?

Ireland's membership of the EEC was negotiated during a lull in the struggle for control of Fianna Fáil. The point of the exaggeration is not the quality of the negotiations but the extent to which the struggle influenced the course of politics since 1970. It changed everything in a way that no other event, or series of events, had done since the party first came to power. It affected how members viewed each other and how outsiders viewed the party; it changed attitudes to leadership and loyalty that had been the hallmarks of Fianna Fáil and made more difficult the achievement of national consensus on issues of national importance. It invaded the party's moments of triumph as well as its periods of turbulence; even its historic victory, in 1977, was accompanied by a sense of foreboding. 'Mr Lynch,' wrote Denis Coghlan in the *Irish Times*, 'just sat there, gazing at the biggest pile of chips ever won by a Fianna Fáil chief.' But as he contemplated his winnings Lynch mournfully remarked that a majority of twenty seats in the Dáil carried with it as many risks as advantages. Sure enough, within two years, the chickens of such huge popularity — in the shape of deputies who felt free to criticise and oppose him — were coming home to roost. Haughey faced the same problem, in reverse, when he became leader and Taoiseach in 1979. His majority over George Colley was so slender that even when Colley made a public declaration of disloyalty to the leaderhsip, he felt he had no option but to ignore it. It took three years —

and three defeated challenges — before Haughey considered himself secure enough to rid the party of those whom he could neither silence nor appease. Colley was now dead. O'Malley, one of Lynch's ablest and most aggressive defenders, was to be expelled. Gibbons was no longer in the Dáil. What remained of the faction that had opposed Haughey had been reduced to impotence. But the ghost of 1970 had not been laid: fifteen years later, O'Malley with the assistance of Mary Harney, an articulate and courageous backbench deputy who had been expelled for opposing Haughey's policy on the North, was preparing the ground for a new challenge, this time from outside the party.

The lull in the struggle for control of Fianna Fáil in the early 'seventies did not mean that the period was uneventful. Far from it. Not only was membership of the EEC negotiated, largely by Hillery and Lynch; there were continuing discussions with often unhelpful — and occasionally dismissive — British leaders on the North. Lynch's aim was to have Britain accept that the Republic had a legitimate interest in the North's affairs and should be regarded as a second guarantor of the rights of the nationalist section of the community. By Fianna Fáil standards it was a modest demand, eminently reasonable and clearly in line with a gradualist approach to unity. Edward Heath, whose arrival in office coincided with a bloody-minded curfew imposed on the Falls Road area of Belfast, took the view that the North was none of the Republic's business and at first refused to discuss it. Harold Wilson, Heath's Labour predecessor — and, indeed, his successor — in Downing Street, liked to boast that he had settled the free trade agreement over a beer and a sandwich in 1965 (which wasn't true) and often told Irish leaders that he had more Irish voters in his Liverpool constituency than they had in theirs. Unlike Wilson, Heath set out with little interest in Irish affairs, considered the North an avoidable distraction and looked on Southern politicians with suspicion. During the period in which he and Lynch headed their respective governments, Anglo-Irish relations were more rancorous than at any time until Haughey and Margaret Thatcher fell out over the H-Blocks hunger strike and the Falklands war. Lynch condemned one-sided internment in 1971 and initiated Ireland's case against Britain at the European Commission and Court of Human Rights; he withdrew the Irish Ambassador from London after the murders of Bloody Sunday in January 1972 had left the country reeling in shock and disbelief. (No one was greatly surprised when, after days of mourning and noisier demonstrations, buildings used by the British Embassy in Dublin were burned down.) Three months later, however, Stormont was prorogued and Heath had come to accept the Republic's interest in Northern affairs; a British discussion document spoke of 'an Irish dimension' in the autumn of 1972. The first steps had been taken towards Sunningdale where, with the Irish and British governments, the Unionists and the SDLP set their seal on the establishment of a power-sharing executive. At Sunningdale, John Hume was overheard to say that Lynch should have been there to witness the signing of an agreement he had worked to produce. Lynch, however, was by then in opposition: he had called a general election in February 1973 in the expectation that security, Northern policy and EEC membership would see the party through. He was also depending on the fragmentation of Fine Gael and the inability of Fine Gael and Labour to find grounds for coalescing. Fine Gael did not fragment, a coalition deal was done and the economy — not the North or security — turned out to be the issue uppermost in people's minds. So that when Liam Cosgrave led the Irish team to Sunningdale, Lynch was no longer in a position to enjoy Heath's conversion, on which he had bet against the odds and which was now expressed in an agreement providing, among other things, that if a majority in the North favoured unity, Britain would do nothing to hinder it. Ironically, when the agreement was presented to the Dáil, Lynch found himself out-manoeuvred and the party, taking its customary swerve into the greenery of opposition, supported an anti-partitionist amendment proposed by Neil Blaney. Though Blaney had already been expelled and Kevin Boland had quit to establish Aontacht Éireann, though Haughey gazed down from the back benches, silent and alone, the vote on Sunningdale was a reminder to the forgetful that the lull was no more than a lull. The struggle for control had been interrupted, not finally decided.

Some commentators thought it odd that Fianna Fáil, with its emphasis on sovereignty and its resistance to outside interference, should have led the campaign for membership of the EEC. Not only did it lead the campaign, it had as its senior ally the 'faithless fellows' of Fine Gael; and to add to the peculiarity, the entry negotiations were conducted in tandem with the age-old enemy, Britain. In fact, it was no more curious than that the proponents of self-sufficiency should go out in search of foreign investment or that the keepers of the republican grail – with the exception of a vociferous minority – should prefer negotiation with Britain to intervention in the North. It was part of a process of modernisation on which the State and the party had embarked; and if there was an air of unreality about the debate, it was because the opposition was so small and the promise of prosperity so tempting. An audience, willing to be awed by the prospect of manna, refused to question the promise or to take the opposition seriously.

During the EEC campaign and again in the 'eighties, the shadowy policy of neutrality became, briefly, the focus of attention. It's a shadowy policy because it has never been satisfactorily defined; neutrality is one of the national pieties to which politicians of all shades attach themselves with sentimental fervour, especially when they are in opposition. Fianna Fáil, crediting de Valera with exclusive authorship of the policy, claims a proprietorial right to it. But even as negotiations which preceded the announcement of neutrality were in progress, de Valera was acknowledging its con-

131

ditional nature. Benevolent neutrality, he argued, would serve both Britain and Ireland best; and, though he carried appearances to the extent of sympathising with the Germans on the death of Hitler, he ensured there was a high degree of co-operation with Britain and the United States during the war. Essentially the argument for neutrality was that the government could not co-operate militarily with any government whose forces continued to occupy part of Ireland's national territory. What might happen, should unity be achieved, was not made clear. During and since de Valera's time, there have been occasional references to the possibility of a bi-lateral pact with Britain. During and since the negotiation of EEC membership, the issue has been further confused by arguments about the nature and extent of Ireland's Community obligations. Lemass said in 1962: 'We recognise that a military commitment will be an inevitable consequence of our joining the Common Market and ultimately we would be prepared to yield even the technical label of neutrality.' In 1969, Lynch took a more cautious view, but noted that we had no tradition of neutrality such as there was in Sweden, Switzerland and Austria and said we would 'naturally be interested in the defence of the territories embraced by the communities — there is no question of neutrality there.' Haughey, who was suspected of offering to trade neutrality for an Anglo-Irish settlement at his meeting with Thatcher in December 1980, argued that full political union of the EEC States would mean the end of Irish neutrality; in the event of unity in Ireland, defence arrangements for the whole island would have to be reviewed. It was what, by then, had become the conventional, conditional view. However, during the elections of 1981 and 1982 and in the course of the Falklands war, Haughey's suspicion of Fine Gael and hostility towards Thatcher led him to harden the conventional line into something that was less benevolent and less conditional: a subtle, but perceptible, shift that was to become part of a pattern — it included decisions on social issues, the New Ireland Forum's report and the Anglo-Irish agreement of November 1985 — obviously designed to satisfy the demands of the political fundamentalists who had put him in control of the party.

Since its period in opposition in the 'seventies, Fianna Fáil had shown signs of movement to the right. Colley, as spokesman on finance, mounted a long and tenacious campaign against the Coalition's modest programme of capital taxation, managing to create an impression that, far from being a feeble attempt at equity, it was a virulent attack on property and personal resources. The party, with the help Cosgrave and some of his colleagues, defeated an attempt to legislate for family planning — a service to which, the Supreme Court decided, citizens had a right. Its attitude to taxation, a curious twist for the party of the open-necked shirts, not only confirmed its traditional support in the construction industry but attracted the financial and psychological support of merchants, entrepreneurs and rich farmers who had become disillusioned with Fine Gael. On family planning, it won the approval of Catholic fundamentalists who were anxious to ensure that if there were change — and the court's decision made that inevitable — it would be of the most limited kind. In government, it was to introduce a ludicrously restrictive measure — Haughey's Irish solution to an Irish problem — which simply dotted the i's and crossed the t's of the bishops' prescription. Ireland's Tory party, as its left-wing critics called it, was really Christian Democratic at heart.

The party had never given much thought to women's affairs and, although de Valera's 'old team' and early national executives benefited from the work of a radical group of women activists, once that group had died or departed, women were to be found in its ranks only in minor roles or as the inheritors of some male relative's political legacy. In 1973, the party had one woman deputy; ten years later, it had four. At the last count, it had three. By the 'seventies, too, its earlier concern with social affairs had been reduced to keeping an electoral

133

eye on the needs of welfare recipients. The nationalists who travelled north when fighting broke out talked long and loudly about the conditions being endured by 'our people in the ghettoes'. Their patriotic zeal had suddenly given them an insight that had, somehow, been missing when they failed to spot the deprivation of the ghettoes on their own doorsteps. Far-away ghettoes are always greener.

For all that, the party in opposition strengthened its organisation and did wonders with its image. Tommy Mullins, de Valera's old comrade in arms, finally retired as general secretary and was replaced by Seamus Brennan, a deceptively easy-going young accountant, who was given the task of weeding out the inefficient and toning up the active bits of the party. How he managed his directors of elections — and, through them exercised a certain control over candidates — became the subject of a television film which other party managers studied with envy. He did it with style, having watched American political operators at close quarters, and with a degree of ruthlessness which took some of the candidates by surprise. But it was Brennan's job to see that his political train ran on time, and that the cheerleaders were there when it arrived; its destination was a matter for Lynch and the committees of politicians, academics and business friends co-ordinated by a gentlemanly lawyer, Esmonde Smyth, who drafted policy documents. The most influential member of the group was Lynch's adviser, Martin O'Donoghue. The party's press relations were handled with great enthusiasm and efficiency by Frank Dunlop, a journalist who had once worked for RTE and canvassed for Labour.

The influence of this set of officials and advisers was greatly resented by people to whom intellectuals, academics, outsiders and youth represented nothing less than a betrayal of old ways and old days. That their energy — or, indeed, a new outlook — might be needed was only grudgingly admitted. But the party had fared badly in five by-elections in a row between 1973 and 1975 and the re-arrangement of con-

stituencies devised by Jim Tully for the Coalition was generally regarded as having eliminated any chance of a Fianna
Fáil victory. People talked longingly about the party's two
efforts to change the voting system in 1959 and 1968, when
proposals to replace proportional representation with the
straight vote had been defeated. One of the reasons behind
those proposals had been the danger of an 'Italian situation' —
governments changing every few months with a proliferation
of small parties and unstable coalitions undermining the
economy and allowing undesirable elements to gain a toehold
in the State. Now, it looked as if the Coalition might last forever. The opinion polls, which Brennan had commissioned,
showed Fianna Fáil well ahead of the combined opposition
forces; but, against the evidence of the by-elections and the
assumption of a successful Tullymander, the polls didn't
stand a chance. A series of Coalition blunders — a heavy-
handed approach to security, the President's resignation
because of a crass insult by a Minister, a bullying speech by
the Taoiseach to the Fine Gael ard-fheis — merely added to
the gap that unemployment, inflation and a tough Budget
had opened up; but Fianna Fáil, the public and the observers
remained unconvinced.

It was only after a week or so in their constituencies that
some leading members of the party began to discover that
their own propaganda was working. By then it was too late
— they had pledged themselves to a manifesto which, along
with some perfectly respectable promises and worthy aspirations, contained the most expensive electioneering bargains
in the history of the State. The package is best remembered
for the bargains — rates off houses, tax off cars — but it also
included a strategy for jobs based on foreign borrowing,
government spending and private enterprise. (It gambled
twice — on growth in world trade and restraint in wage demands at home — and on both counts it lost.) On the night
before polling, I met Colley walking through Leinster Lawn
and asked him what he thought of the criticisms the mani-

festo had provoked. 'I think', he said, 'we've done just enough to stay in touch.' Even Lynch, who'd been predicting '77 seats in the year of 77' seemed surprised when, two days later, he sat gazing at the biggest haul ever achieved by a Fianna Fáil leader: 84 seats in a House of 148 deputies. He rewarded Martin O'Donoghue with a new Department of his own, Economic Planning and Development; and O'Donoghue, a man of cherubic innocence and genuine charm, immediately promised to eliminate unemployment. It hasn't stopped rising since.

The party, for the time being, was the organisation with everything: secure financial support, a lively youth section (mostly Brennan's work), a crop of ambitious new deputies and the approval, so far as could be discovered, of a majority of those who had voted for the first time (perhaps, one quarter of the electorate). But its victory precipitated a change in the leadership of Fine Gael, which was to have deep and lasting effects on that party, while raising the possibility of renewed turbulence within its own ranks. The more backbenchers there are in a parliamentary party, the more disappointed politicians the party's leader will have on his hands; and if there is an alternative leader waiting in the wings, ready to plug in to the power-house of their discontent, trouble is inevitable. In a party like Fianna Fáil, which places such emphasis on leadership and has as one of its enduring legacies the old, dark fear of a split, the threat grows like a fist of cloud in a wintry sky.

Haughey, in a moment of euphoria following his acquittal in 1970, called on those responsible for 'this debâcle' — by which he meant his dismissal and trial — to 'take the course open to them'. He didn't mention Lynch or resignation, and he did not return to the subject during the years of his rehabilitation, but neither did he lower his sights from the ambition he had publicly set himself in 1966. To achieve it he was prepared to endure humiliation on the back benches, voting with and for his accusers in the Dáil, and to undertake a tour of the country that was half pilgrimage and half recruiting drive, motoring alone or with some helpful friend to towns and villages he once would not have visited without the accompaniment of a band. He told James Downey, the author of *Them and Us*, how he could identify the factories from which the inevitable chicken came; but never, at any of those dinners on what Downey calls the 'rubber chicken circuit' did he permit himself the luxury of a sentence, publicly uttered, which could be considered disloyal. Making common cause with those who, for one reason or another, did not hold party office, or with officers who were out of favour with headquarters, as well as with any local representatives who cared to meet him — and very many did — he crossed the familiar territory again and again and sat and smiled and waited. Vice-president, joint honorary secretary, spokesman and Minister, he advanced step by step on his goal with impatience that he admitted only to his friends. He watched and noted — and saw to it that others noted — the by-election failures; he wryly observed Lynch's lapse of memory in the case of the Littlejohns, two Englishmen who claimed to have been British agents engaged in provocative actions in the Republic — Lynch did not recall being told about them — and in the Dáil he said nothing at all. His appointment to the front bench in 1975 coincided with a stiffening of Northern policy, which was curiously foreshadowed — a few days in advance — by another front-bencher, Michael O'Kennedy. Lynch was annoyed by O'Kennedy's speech suggesting that Britain should declare her intention of withdrawing from the North but publicly denied that anything more than a shift in emphasis was involved. He told colleagues who asked him about Haughey's promotion that he believed there was a demand for it in the party. Among others, Gibbons privately objected and later claimed to have been given an assurance by Haughey that he would clear his name of an accusation implicit in Haughey's evidence at the arms trial. To have done so, Haughey would have had to admit

137

that he had committed perjury. As on all other aspects of the arms trial, Haughey chose to remain silent.

Haughey's appointment as Minister for Health and Social Welfare was taken for granted. When Lynch was asked about it in 1985 he repeated what he and most other contributors to the 1970 debate had said: that Haughey had been, before his fall, a brilliant Minister with a great future ahead of him. To this Lynch now added that he thought it would be unfair — unjust and un-Christian — to continue to penalise Haughey. In the years since the trial, he had not proved himself disloyal. But consciousness of the size and troublesome potential of his new majority can hardly have failed to play some part in the Taoiseach's decision. Haughey, for his part, took charge of two big and difficult Departments without assistance, with every sign of his old capacity for hard work and flair for publicity. He paid special attention to the cases brought to him by backbenchers, impressed his civil servants with his quick and clear decisions, and he kept himself in the public eye, as much by devising inexpensive but ingenious schemes as by making major announcements. But neither old enmities nor his real ambition lay dormant for long. Gibbons, once more a cabinet colleague, refused to support his Family Planning Bill on conscientious grounds and, after some huffing and puffing about whether or not he might be forced to resign, was given his way. It was the first and only time that the party allowed anything approaching a free vote. Then, as public service strikes made life increasingly difficult for the government, Haughey offered to help in the case of some postal workers whose long and bitter strike was one of the most debilitating labour disputes in Ireland since the war.

The government had run into trouble on several fronts. PAYE taxpayers took to the streets in greater numbers than ever before to demand movement towards equity. They were made even angrier by a chance remark of Colley's, which seemed to belittle their claims, and by the abandonment of a farm levy after protests by the farmers. A minor but highly irritating oil crisis was provoked by a disagreement between O'Malley (now in Industry and Commerce) and the oil companies. With unemployment reaching 110,000 Lynch was reminded that he had said soon after arriving in office that if it topped 100,000 the Taoiseach should resign. He, in turn, blamed private enterprise for not having produced the jobs the country needed in spite of the government's pump-priming as promised in its manifesto. He was, in any event, preoccupied with negotiations to take the Republic into the European Monetary System and out of the sterling area during much of 1978 and with Ireland's presidency of the EEC in the second half of 1979.

Haughey watched and waited with increasing impatience as the party put in a feeble performance in the European and local elections in mid-summer, 1979. At the end of August, Lynch was in London for the funeral of Mountbatten, who had been murdered by the Provisional IRA near his home at Mullaghmore in Sligo, and Thatcher, who had been elected in May, used the occasion to demand closer co-operation between the British and Irish governments on Border security. The British had for some time been seeking an agreement which would allow them to cross the Border in hot pursuit of suspects fleeing from the North. Reports in the British media, some of which seemed to blame Lynch for the murder of a senior member of the Royal family, now returned to the theme and for more than a month there was speculation as to what London was demanding of Dublin and what Dublin was prepared to concede. An authoritative report by Michael Mills in the *Irish Press* spoke of an air corridor which would allow limited surveillance on either side of the Border. The idea was bound to inflame opinion in a party that had been worried by the election results and irked by the tone of many of the British commentaries on Mountbatten. But Haughey's stalking horses were already on the move. Without any public endorsement by their faction leader, over twenty of them had taken part in a caucus meeting in Leinster House, ostensibly to discuss the implications of the election results; their real target was Lynch. Then Sile de Valera used the deeply symbolic occasion of the annual Liam Lynch commemoration to attack the party leader's Northern policy. Standing at the grave of the IRA Chief of Staff who had been killed in the final days of the Civil War, she left no one in doubt that she thought Jack Lynch had departed from the line approved by her grandfather. Anticipating trouble with Lynch, she had taken the precaution of distributing her script to the newspapers and RTE before being called to his office to discuss it. The speech was gratuitously damaging, especially in view of the gradualism de Valera had come to adopt towards the end of his active career and the opinions he had expressed to O'Malley about the 1970 crisis and the North.

Haughey made only one public contribution to the whole debate. That was on 10 November, three days after Lynch had begun a tour of the United States that was to be punctuated by bad news from home. On 8 November came the report that the party had lost two by-elections in Cork city and county. Next day at the Washington Press Club he inadvertently confirmed the report that British flights over Border areas had been permitted but claimed that no change of policy was involved. That weekend, Bill Loughnane of Clare accused him of lying and Colley undertook the task of seeing that Loughnane was expelled from the parliamentary party. The move failed. The news that Haughey at last had spoken was broken to Lynch as he prepared to leave Boston for New Orleans. A copy of the speech had been sent by telex and was being anxiously studied by the official party at the back of the US Air Force plane as it headed south. Dunlop passed it on to the political correspondents, none of whom thought it amounted to much. All I can remember now was that it contained, with a lot of Haughey's usual rhetoric, a single reference to Pearse. 'You have to know the code,' said Seán Duignan of RTE, a man wiser than most in the ways of the party. 'They're sending semaphore messages to each other across the Atlantic. The people in the back know what it means and they don't like it.' When Lynch moved on to the Regal Ranch outside Houston next day, I found the temptation irresistible and sent home a piece saying that the Taoiseach was meeting some real cowboys for a change. No sooner had he returned to Dublin than the Haugheyites were planning a petition for his resignation. Colley and O'Donoghue advised him that a quick contest would suit them best and, on 5 December, a month earlier than he had planned, he announced his departure. Liam Cosgrave's tribute to 'the most popular Irish politician since Daniel O'Connell' reflected opinion outside, if not within, the party.

Haughey was in ebullient mood. He believed (rightly, as it happened) that a short, sharp campaign would suit him best. He had done his homework. There were few backbenchers who did not owe him a favour of some sort and he felt he could exert influence over three or four members of the cabinet as well. He totted them up as he sat in his office with friends and allies only hours after Lynch had made his announcement, and came to the conclusion that he'd have 58 votes to Colley's 24. Rubbing his hands, he looked around the company for confirmation. There were three westerners in the room. Seán Doherty of Roscommon, Tom McEllistrim of Kerry and Mark Killilea of Galway, with Charlie McCreevy of Kildare; all of them had been active in the caucus that had campaigned against Lynch. McCreevy was its secretary, but it was Doherty who, after a moment's mental arithmetic, laughingly commented on Haughey's estimate: 'Do you know, you're the worst fucking judge of people I ever met.' Doherty was right.

Colley's campaign managers were just as confident and even more unrealistic. Some of Haughey's supporters who infiltrated the opposition camp, either to find out what was going on or to give the others a false sense of security, found that they were accepted without question. The opinion that Colley would win handsomely was shared by several members of the cabinet who had canvassed no more than a handful of backbenchers.

The electioneering continued for forty-eight hours. A respected political scientist reported: 'There was a certain amount of last-minute switching of allegiance, and a lot of pressure, not all of it exactly gracefully applied, was experienced by uncommitted deputies and even by members of the factions. There is a good deal of evidence of vote-trading, and there were strong rumours of bribery and of what amounted to direct intimidation: the atmosphere in Leinster House before the vote was sulphurous. To put it in a minimal fashion, there was a concerted attempt, by the use of rumour, to represent a Haughey victory as inevitable and to generate a bandwagon effect by stampeding uncommitted TDs into voting for him.'

Haughey wanted to be proposed by a member of the cabinet, but only Brian Lenihan, his old companion of the mohair-suited days in the Russell Hotel, was thought likely to back him; and Haughey's lieutenants may have remembered that, when everyone was taking sides back in 1970, Lenihan was quoted as having said that he was like the X in OXO. (He was later to say that he had canvassed support for Lynch.) Haughey asked his lieutenants to look for someone else. Eventually, they settled on Ray MacSharry, who was not a member of the cabinet but a junior minister who'd been promoted by Lynch and served in Colley's department. On the eve of the poll, Michael O'Kennedy who had been keeping a lonely vigil in his office — just in case the party, at the last minute, might have wished to avoid a divisive contest — let it be known that he was prepared to back Haughey. The campaign managers, who had shrewdly judged what a close-run thing it would be, guessed that O'Kennedy would influence the decisions of, perhaps, a couple of Munster deputies. Their votes would be crucial, so it was all-important that they be delivered. Colley's camp was flattened by the news. Long afterwards, O'Malley, seeing O'Kennedy's European Commission limousine pass by, was heard to mutter: 'Judas's chariot'.

In spite of their calculations and all those promised votes, no one could be quite sure how the election would go in the party's big committee room in Leinster House on Friday, 7 December. Some of Haughey's team positioned themselves near the door the better to observe: MacSharry, as the proposer, was the teller on their side and would be the first to know the result. If they'd been successful, he would turn in their direction and raise his right hand. The count, as the votes were checked and double-checked, seemed to go on forever. Then MacSharry turned around. In the crush, he could not raise his hand as high as he had intended. But he was able to get it up to his face, and he slowly rubbed his right eye. It was enough. They knew.

11

Appealing to the Past

Haughey was more concerned with savouring success than with mending fences. He had achieved his ambition against all the odds and in a surprisingly short time. Little more than nine years and seven months separated his ignominious departure from office and his arrival as leader and Taoiseach. Nothing, not even the need to protect the party's fragile unity, would be allowed to interfere with his sense of triumph. He walked like a man whose feet barely touched the ground.

He dismissed, though he could neither forgive nor forget, an unfortunate and unexplained reference by Garret FitzGerald in the Dáil to his 'flawed pedigree'. He chose to ignore more cutting speeches, in one of which Frank Cluskey, the Labour leader, said that Haughey's ambition was to own Ireland; in another, Noel Browne compared him with the Portuguese dictator, Antonio Salazar. His supporters, however, were in no mood to let these taunts pass though the real begrudgers, as far as they were concerned, sat in the government's benches around them. They took their revenge by boasting of — and exaggerating — the role they'd played in Lynch's departure. It was the first time that any party's backbenchers had succeeded in having their own man installed in leadership against the wishes of all but a couple of their Ministers; and reconciliation was the last thing on their minds. 'He should have sacked the lot,' they told each other and any of their dazed opponents who cared to listen.

Haughey's attempts at bridge-building were short-lived,

tentative and unsuccessful. His majority over Colley was six. Three years later, when he fought off the third assault on his leadership, his majority was seven, though in a smaller party. His suspicions and their resentment made relations with leading members of the opposing faction difficult to maintain even when they were not plotting against him. Gradually, he came to fill every vacancy that arose with his own supporters and to surround himself with officials and advisers who could be relied on to agree with him. On arrival in office, he dispensed with the services of two of Lynch's Ministers — Jim Gibbons, his old adversary from the arms trial, and Martin O'Donoghue, the author of much of the 1977 manifesto, whose separate Department of Economic Planning and Development he scornfully dissolved. He made a deal with Colley involving a veto on appointments to the security departments, Justice and Defence, but blundered by announcing that he had won Colley's loyalty along with his agreement to serve in the new cabinet. Colley, who had agreed with reluctance to take a post, was incensed; and in a speech delivered in Baldoyle, Co. Dublin less than a fortnight after Haughey's election he made a declaration which, at any other time or in any other circumstance, would have led to his instant dismissal: 'A majority of the parliamentary party has, it seems to me, at least for the life of the present parliamentary party, changed the traditional Fianna Fáil rule and legitimised the withholding of loyalty to, and support for, the elected leader. I very much regret this but I am a realist and I accept it.' Colley was prepared to serve Haughey as Taoiseach; he no longer felt obliged to be loyal to him as leader. Such a change would have been unthinkable when de Valera or Lemass controlled the party. Even at the nadir of the arms crisis, when Lynch's leadership was under threat, no one dared say so in such unequivocal terms. Now, it was clear that unquestioning loyalty and unassailable leadership were things of the past; and, curiously, while it caused some tension in the cabinet, there was no public recrimination. It had the air of a local row.

Haughey made one other public effort to come to terms with his critics. In January 1980 he went on television to deliver a state-of-the-nation address which concentrated on the economy. The terse, business-like style he had learned from his father-in-law, Seán Lemass, matched the occasion and the message: we were living beyond our means, borrowing too much, especially from foreign sources, and spending too much on day-to-day administration; we simply could not afford to go on paying ourselves more than we earned. Moderation was the key to success. Des O'Malley telephoned Colley after the broadcast and said there were promising signs that the new man — O'Malley rarely spoke of Haughey by name — was getting things right. Colley's reply was a snort of disbelief. Exactly six years later O'Malley was in the throes of setting up a new party whose diagnosis of the State's economic ills followed roughly the lines of Haughey's broadcast. Haughey, however, had taken off within months of the broadcast in quite a different direction, reminding anyone who complained about it that he had an election to win.

Some refused to take him seriously, believing that he was too shrewd a businessman, too wily a politician to fall for the obvious traps. Others convinced themselves that he really did intend to hold an early election, for he behaved like a leader who wanted the whole country to celebrate his acquisition of power. Colleagues who had heartily approved of his broadcast analysis of the State's economic and financial problems nervously recalled a remark he'd made in the 'sixties: 'A million? Sure you'd lose it in a tot.' It was a joke in the golden years when the economy and the mohair-suited men were riding high. In the middle of the second recession in a decade, it had an ominous ring: Haughey acted as if these were the free-wheeling 'sixties when political strokes were greatly admired and everyone thought that someone else was footing the bill. It was the generation of the cute hoor, of whom Haughey was the cutest. As Minister for Finance he'd managed a series of small but much appreciated advances for the old and the infirm and introduced a generous concession to writers and artists that brought him international acclaim; it was to other, more complicated manoeuvres that the tag 'cute hoor' applied. As Taoiseach he seemed to believe that it was up to him to go on upstaging colleagues and outwitting opponents in a way that surpassed his earlier reputation: the 'sixties man made promises (Knock Airport) that the cabinet knew nothing about, cut across Ministers (teachers' pay) to win over sections of the electorate, announced the rescue of industries or the building of hospitals on the spur of the moment. He outwitted FitzGerald with a scheme for Dublin's inner city (the Gregory deal) to secure the support of a crucial Independent and fell into his own trap when he handed the European Commissioner's job to a member of the opposition (Dick Burke), then failed to win the by-election that he'd caused.

The party in the first half of the 'eighties revolved around Haughey. He dominated its affairs in a way that no other leader had done; in the style of an East European head of state whose basilisk stare follows his citizens wherever they go, he spoke for all on every issue of importance and was quick to detect any hint of dissent. In a book published in 1972, Conor Cruise O'Brien wrote: 'I thought that, if conditions ever became ripe for a characteristically Irish Catholic form of dictatorship, Charles J. Haughey would make a plausible enough Taoiseach/Duce.' Twelve years later, Haughey's press secretary, P. J. Mara, inadvertently echoed the observation when he said, in an aside never intended for publication, that in Fianna Fáil it was a case of *uno Duce, una voce.* Haughey was not amused. He had always paid obsessive attention to anything that was written about him, believing that in the most innocent piece of reportage there was some hidden message of praise or blame. Even the position of a report or photograph could be significant. 'What's this?' he was heard to say, as he opened his copy of the *Irish Press* one morning. 'Nice picture of you, Taoiseach,' one of his assistants replied. 'Yes, but where is it?' said Haughey. 'In the *Irish Press*,' the assistant said, 'it's in the *Irish Press*, page three.' 'Page three! And where should it be?' 'On page one, Taoiseach. It should be on page one.' Most political leaders merely skim the day's papers. The Taoiseach, as a rule, is presented with a summary of their contents. Cosgrave read little and rarely spoke to anyone about what they'd written; Haughey could be driven into a fury by a report or comment, hated being contradicted in any way and believed that all criticism of him was inspired by malice. When, in 1982, his minority government was rocked again and again by the series of events that came to be characterised as GUBU — grotesque, unbelievable, bizarre and unprecedented, the words he had used to describe the arrest of a murderer who had been staying with his attorney-general — he and some of his friends were inclined to see the hand of the British secret service in their misfortune.

The party, under his leadership, looked to the past for inspiration. To the 'sixties, as we have seen, on questions of tactics and style; to the 'fifties, on relations between Church and State; to the 'twenties, on the North. It called for discipline of a kind that had never before been enforced and such obedience to the leader as even de Valera had never demanded. But, then, de Valera did not have to fight three elections in eighteen months or to meet the fierce internal opposition that Haughey faced. For if he was the first leader to have been imposed by the backbenchers, he was also the first to have been openly refused loyalty by his colleagues and consistently rejected by one-quarter of those who voted for the party. The three attempts to remove him from leadership were part of the continuing struggle for control, symptomatic of divisions that had had their origins in the 'sixties and came to a head in 1970. The first attempt began while the party was still smarting from its defeat in the 1981 election and gained momentum when it failed to win an overall majority in the first election of 1982. Ominously, the opening shots were fired by Charlie McCreevy, one of the

148

most energetic Haugheyites in the campaign against Lynch. In an interview with Geraldine Kennedy, then political correspondent of the *Sunday Tribune*, he was severely critical of politics and politicians generally and of Haughey in particular. The main target of his attack was the irresponsibility of all sides in dealing with the nation's finances, but McCreevy was also plainly disillusioned with Haughey's refusal to come to grips with his defeat in '81. When the '82 results became known, others joined in: with McCreevy forcing the pace, Colley, Gibbons and O'Malley, encouraged by Bobby Molloy of Galway, another of Lynch's Ministers, decided that they should challenge Haughey's re-election when the new parliamentary party met. O'Malley was to be their candidate. But their organisation was poor and some people from whom they had expected support, O'Donoghue for example, argued that now was not the time to make a stand. No-one was quite sure whether or not the party would be able to form the next government. Discouraged by such talk and by defections from his camp, O'Malley allowed himself to be persuaded by some of the party's elders that in the interest of unity he should withdraw.

Nineteen eighty-two was the worst year in the party's history. The tone was set by the Gregory deal, details of which were unknown to most of Haughey's colleagues until the Independent Dublin deputy read them to the Dáil. There followed a series of scandals, policy changes and misadventures, some self-inflicted injuries and entirely accidental occurrences, which did much to damage not only Fianna Fáil and its leader but politics and politicians in the eyes of an already sceptical electorate. The year has been described in clinical style and with professional competence by Joe Joyce and Peter Murtagh in *The Boss*. By October it was clear that the government was not going to survive and when, on the first day of the month, McCreevy tabled a motion of no confidence in Haughey, the only surprise was that the dissidents were going to stick their necks out again. This time,

McCreevy was acting on his own. The first O'Malley heard of the challenge was when his secretary in the Department of Industry and Commerce telephoned him in Spain: 'Minister, I thought you might like to know . . .' But McCreevy's independent action forced the hands of both O'Malley and O'Donoghue, the leading dissidents in the cabinet; they refused to grant Haughey the support he demanded of all Ministers and resigned on the night before the meeting at which the motion was to be discussed. That was 'the night of the long telephone calls' during which Haughey's lieutenants, the north-western triumvirate of MacSharry, Seán Doherty and Albert Reynolds, contacted deputies all over the country to inquire how they intended to vote. It was the first indication that the threat was being taken seriously. Other messages were delivered that night which were not simple inquiries. In one case, a racehorse trainer who was a substantial contributor to party funds made the call; in another, it was a hotel owner in a southern town; a third call was made by a businessman who had dealings with a deputy engaged in manufacturing industry. The messages were similar: the callers were leaning on their local representatives to 'do the right thing'. Subscriptions, services and business deals were at stake. Promotions were promised to some wavering backbenchers, others were reminded of favours they had enjoyed. Friends, families and relatives were contacted and asked to exert their influence on stubborn TDs. One country deputy telephoned his wife and was told that several men had been sitting for hours outside the house, waiting to talk to him; neighbours in the resort where he had a holiday home called later to say that a carload of men was waiting for him there, too. Next day, Haughey insisted on an open vote and McCreevy's motion was defeated by 58 votes to 22.

The final assault on Haughey's leadership came in January 1983, six weeks after his government had been defeated. Michael Noonan, the newly elected Minister for Justice, announced that Seán Doherty, Noonan's predecessor, had initiated taps on the phones of two political journalists, Geraldine Kennedy and Bruce Arnold (of the *Irish Independent*), in a quite unorthodox fashion and that Garda equipment had been supplied by Doherty to MacSharry to 'bug' a conversation he'd had with O'Donoghue about financial affairs — in particular, MacSharry's and Haughey's. Within days, the Garda Commissioner and Assistant Commissioner, Patrick McLaughlin and Joe Ainsworth, had resigned; MacSharry and Doherty had quit the front bench and the parliamentary party had set up an internal inquiry into the whole affair. In a year of scandals it was one of the most scandalous events: the excuse for tapping the journalists' phones — that information from cabinet meetings was getting into their papers — was feeble in the extreme. Taps are supposed to be initiated only in cases where serious crime or national security is involved. The bugging of MacSharry's conversation with O'Donoghue was justified on the grounds that O'Donoghue was attempting to suggest that financial assistance might be used to influence the party's choice of leader. The propriety of bugging colleagues' conversations was ignored or, at any rate, submerged in the tide of outrage that the notion of financial influence provoked. John Bowman, discussing the affair with O'Donoghue on RTE, described it as an ethical minefield. O'Donoghue agreed, but ethics do not loom large on the political horizon and when Doherty and O'Donoghue both offered their resignations to the parliamentary party they were accepted with undiscriminating relief. Doherty quietly returned to the party in 1985, with Haughey's blessing; MacSharry went on to win a seat in the European Parliament in the same year, after which he came to be regarded as a potential challenger for leadership. Other challengers had emerged during the crisis of '83: O'Malley again, O'Kennedy now back after a brief stint as European Commissioner, Gerry Collins of West Limerick, a crafty operator who had not been crafty enough to prevent Haughey from luring him into the open in the course of a three-week campaign from which no one emerged unscathed. Haughey's interests — and, many thought, Haughey personally — were at the root of Doherty's and MacSharry's troubles. It was he who was concerned about the leaking of information from the cabinet and it was he who was likely to be most affected by rumours about financial difficulties and possible changes of allegiance. His fight to survive, which ranged from a statement suggesting that he might appeal to the ard-fheis over the heads of deputies to delaying and diversionary tactics while he summoned his strength and set his opponents in competition with each other, was a masterly display of resilience and determination. Once he seemed on the point of resigning: a close friend, who was not a politician, emerged from his office to say he was drafting a statement to be delivered to his parliamentary colleagues. If indeed it was written, it was not delivered. On 7 February, a motion requesting his resignation 'now' was defeated by 40 votes to 33. The encouragement of two close associates, Padraig Flynn and Neil Blaney, had helped. So had the failure of his critics to agree on a successor. The party of Taca had taken offence at the suggestion of financial influence; it had made no bones about phone tapping or the bugging of private conversations. Reluctantly, a week later, it carried a resolution condemning all three activities; but by then it was a formality which bothered few of its leading members.

Most commentators looked forward to a fight when Haughey met Thatcher for the first time in May 1980. It was not so much the desired as the expected outcome of a meeting between leaders who were opposites in everything but temperament. What happened was that Haughey presented Thatcher with a Georgian silver teapot and persuaded her to travel to Dublin, six months later, with the most impressive British delegation to have visited Ireland for a very long time. The communiqué issued after the London meeting was bland but friendly; it acknowledged the unique nature of Anglo-Irish relations and the principle of consent — Northern Ireland would remain part of the United Kingdom until a majority of the people of the North decided otherwise, in which case no one would stand in the way of unity. The Dublin meeting was followed by an announcement of joint studies by officials of all aspects of Anglo-Irish relations, including future institutional arrangements. The leaders' next meeting would be about the 'totality of relations' within the islands. Haughey, at press conferences and briefings, began to expound on what that meant: all options were open, he told political correspondents, including constitutional change. Thatcher, on her return to London, was neither as forthcoming nor as optimistic and, with Unionist alarm growing, soon felt compelled to say that nothing out of the ordinary had occurred at Dublin Castle. When next she met Haughey, at an EEC Heads of Government meeting in Holland, she turned on him in fury, complaining that he and his chief spokesman, Lenihan, had exaggerated the progress made in Dublin to the point of distortion. She was not prepared to be helpful to Haughey on the H-Blocks hunger strike, which was already under way and which, he believed, was to cost him two seats in the 1981 election; it was the beginning of the deterioration of a promising relationship which withered completely during the Falklands War. Haughey, who reprimanded Sile de Valera for making an anti-Thatcher speech in his optimistic phase, now led the party into an introspective and crudely anti-British mood which embittered Irish relationships as well. Emphasising the claim that Northern Ireland as a political entity had failed, he refused to have anything to do with attempts at an internal settlement of any kind. He was deeply suspicious of FitzGerald's invitation to join the New Ireland Forum and when it ended with a set of three options in a report declaring the willingness of nationalists to consider every way forward, he chose the narrowest interpretation: a unitary state, soon translated to 'a united Ireland', was not merely the ideal solution, it was the only solution. In this Fianna Fáil disagreed with Fine Gael, Labour and the SDLP, and, within the party, Haughey disagreed profoundly with O'Malley, who demanded that the question should, at least, be discussed before public positions were adopted. Haughey's response was to have him expelled from the parliamentary group; nine months later, O'Malley was expelled from the organisation, formally for abstaining during a vote on contraception, in practice because he had embarrassed Haughey with a speech about Church-State relations which ended with the declaration: 'I stand by the republic.' Haughey went on to take a highly critical — and, as it happened, very unpopular — view of the Anglo-Irish Agreement which was inspired by the Forum and signed by Thatcher and FitzGerald at Hillsborough, Co. Down in November 1985. Three weeks before the agreement was made public, Haughey issued a warning couched in terms clearly intended to remind his audience of the 1922 Treaty and the Civil War. On publication, he modified his rhetoric but not his position though other senior members of the party adopted a less aggressive stance and a few public representatives — most notably, Mary Harney in the Dáil and Eoin Ryan, the son of Jim Ryan, one of de Valera's old team, in the Senate — defied their leader's wishes and backed the agreement. O'Malley chose this moment to announce his new party, the Progressive Democrats. It was the third party to have emerged, directly or indirectly, from the 1970 crisis; and it was the one most likely to succeed.

12

Conclusion

Fianna Fáil set out with the hope of founding a republic and ended up a partitionist party in a twenty-six county State. But those who imagined that it would die or be rejected by the electorate if its deepest ambitions were not achieved are confounded by its strength and resilience as it celebrates the sixtieth anniversary of its foundation. The European and local elections in 1985 proved that it still had the pulling-power which rewarded its efforts from the beginning. I am not saying that the party – or the ground it stands on – remains unchanged. It set out to represent the nation, people of all creeds and classes united in the common bond of Irish-ness. Discovering that that was too ambitious, too awkward and inconvenient an achievement to aim for, it was content to shape the State that it inherited and to be consoled by the thought that there was nothing wrong with the party that was not also wrong with the country.

The best or worst, but certainly most vividly remembered, example of partitionism in practice was the abortion referen-dum of 1983. A law was already on the statute books which made abortion a crime. Though it had not been much used in recent years, that was probably because most women who wanted abortions travelled to Britain for the operation – and the best estimates available were that the numbers were increasing steadily all the time. Fundamentalist organisations, some of them set up specifically for this purpose, others with a longer record in the area of Church-State relations generally, decided that a legal provision was not enough; abortion should be subject to a constitutional prohibition. The implication was clear: a law might be changed by the Oireachtas; the constitution could only be changed by the electorate in a referendum. The elected representatives of the people could not be trusted, so power should be removed from their hands. After meetings with representatives of the Pro-Life Amendment Campaign, the leaders of the three major parties — obviously fearful of being labelled abortionists in the run-up to an election — agreed in 1981 that a referendum should be held. Some Protestant church leaders were, as they put it, dubious about the proposal and it soon became clear that not all Catholics were in favour of the idea. Fianna Fáil in government during 1982 wrestled with the problem of finding appropriate wording for an amendment and, with their defeat imminent, came up with a formula that had been worked out in consultation with a representative of the Catholic Church and the help of a member of the judiciary. FitzGerald at first agreed to it but, with Protestant doubts and fears increasing, changed his mind on arrival in office and, on the advice of his attorney-general, offered an alternative which could be described as minimal: it was less difficult to define and somewhat less contentious than the Fianna Fáil version. The Catholic bishops supported Fianna Fáil's wording, rejected the revision and threw their weight behind the fundamentalists who had not always appeared certain of hierarchical support. Fianna Fáil's view prevailed, with the assistance of many Fine Gael and a few Labour deputies in the Dáil, by a two-to-one majority in the State. Haughey called for a vote in favour of the amendment, FitzGerald announced that he would be voting against and the newly elected Labour leader, Dick Spring, now Tánaiste, claimed that a concerted campaign was being waged with the support of the hierarchy to roll back the tide on social issues.

The two-to-one majority was achieved in a poll of less than 54 per cent, against strong urban opposition (five Dublin con-

constituencies voted 'No' and there were strong 'anti' votes in the cities of Cork, Limerick, Galway and Waterford as well as dormitory areas, Kildare and Meath) and a wave of resentment at the Republic's pretensions to pluralism and its declared interest in unity. There was a very strong relationship between those who voted 'Yes' and support for Fianna Fáil in the November '82 election, according to Michael Gallagher, a political scientist, writing in the *Irish Times*: 'Fianna Fáil supporters seem to have voted fairly solidly in favour of the amendment, and may have formed the majority of those voting "Yes".' It was not the only social issue on which the party now looked to the so-called traditional values, marrying religious and political fundamentalism – the partners of the past – with an eye to electoral opportunity. It opposed the rationalisation of a contraceptive law that was both impractical and unjust; it played political games with divorce – while Fine Gael equivocated, hesitated and lost its nerve – and it continued to regard the tattered remains of FitzGerald's constitutional crusade as if it were revolutionary or subversive or both.

With Fine Gael edging its way towards Fianna Fáil's old position – that of a catch-all party with a reforming edge – Fianna Fáil retreated to the right and, as of old, looked to the past. Not to the sinewy, vaguely anti-clerical organisation which was seen as a threat to the established order in the late 'twenties, but to the place that Fine Gael had so long and so unctuously occupied with its air of clericalism and obedience. The people who cheer loudest at ardfheiseanna – 'Up the Republic' and 'Brits Out' – would be shocked at the suggestion that there has been such a change, but everything they do – as distinct from the things they shout for – confirms it: partitionism with a clerical touch; a party looking to the past in a country increasingly populated by young people with new and different concerns; and, on a different level though there is a link between the two, a party which has failed to win a secure majority in three elections in a row and has been out of office for eight of the past fifteen years.

Our neighbour who knew that there always was a Fianna Fáil and always would be would, I like to think — through the fog and smoke, the excitement and disappointments of the intervening years — say the same today. He'd be right, too, but it might not be the party that he knew.

Index